The KINGSTON BOOK

First published 2006
by Historical Publications Ltd
32 Ellington Street, London N7 8PL
(Tel: 020 7607 1628)

ISBN 1-905286-05-8
British Library Cataloguing-in-Publication Data
A catalogue record for this book is available from the British Library

Reproduction by Liz Morrell and Paddy Donnelly
Printed in Zaragoza, Spain by Edelvives

The Illustrations

The following illustrations are reproduced by kind permission:
Bentall Centre: *17, 18*
Bentalls: *11, 12, 13, 14*
John Blackmore: *100*
Historical Publications Ltd: *9, 40, 52, 53, 56, 59, 65, 93, 105*
Kingston Museum and Heritage Service: *1, 2, 4, 5, 6, 8, 16, 19, 23, 24, 28, 30, 38, 39, 41, 48, 51, 57, 58, 60, 62, 63, 64, 68, 70, 74, 75, 76, 77, 78, 81, 88, 91, 96, 101, 102, 104, 114, 116, 127, 131, 132, 133, 134, 135, 141, 142, 143, 144, 145, 146, 147, 148, 152, 153*
National Monuments Record: *126*
National Portrait Gallery: *54*
Penguin Books: *67*
Random House Children's Books: *154*
Surrey Comet: *15, 36, 94, 97, 98, 99, 130*
Tiffin Boys' School: *150*
Oliver Tims: *112*
Michael Turk: *20*
All other illustrations were supplied by the Author, June Sampson

The KINGSTON BOOK

June Sampson

HISTORICAL PUBLICATIONS

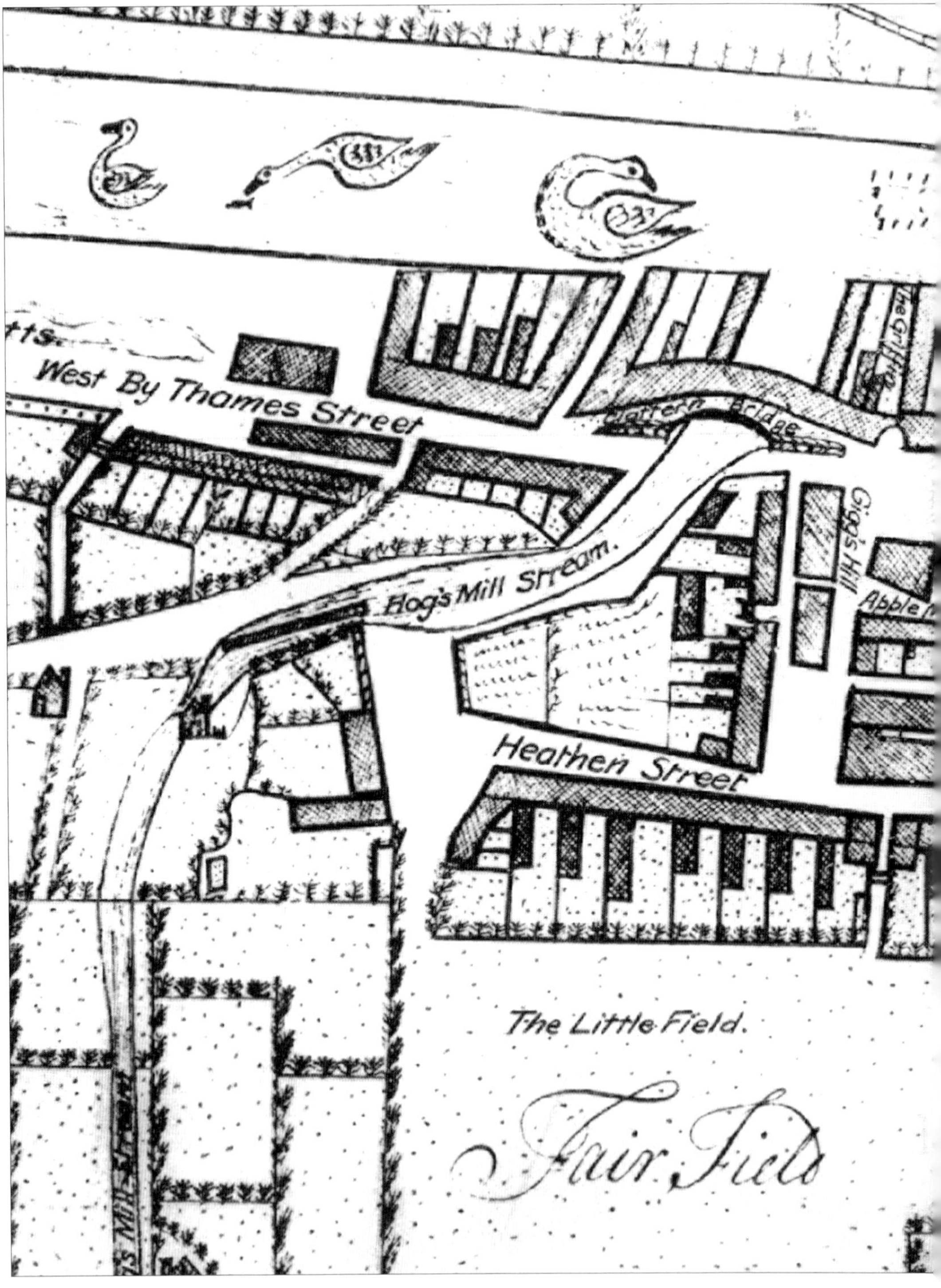

1. A 17th-century plan of central Kingston. Names in type were added later.

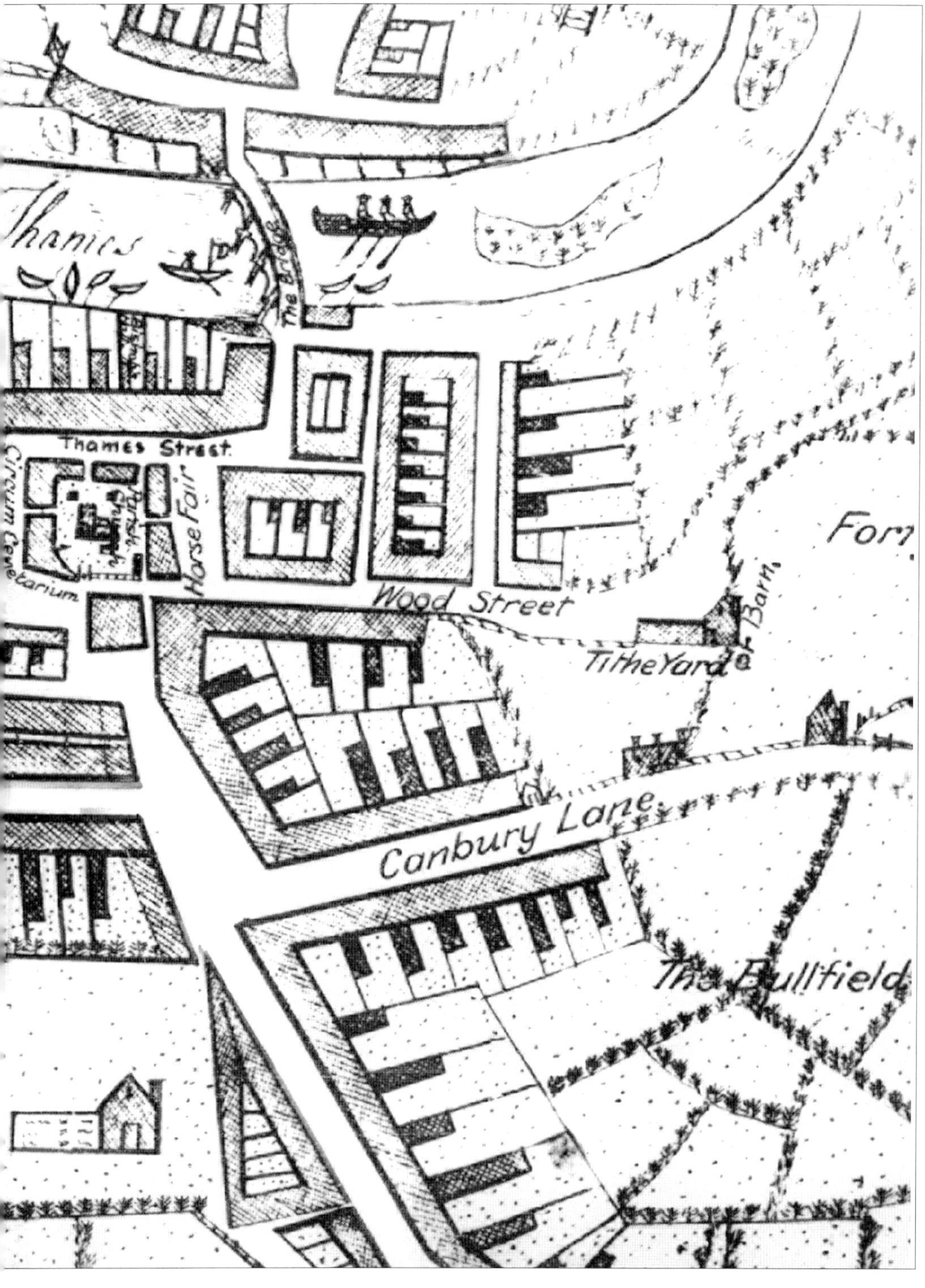
Thames
The Bridge
Thames Street
Circum Cemetarium
Horse Fair
Wood Street
Tithe Yard
Barn
Form
Canbury Lane
The Bullfield

Introduction

Kingston has such a teeming history that one could write a hundred books on it and still have material left over. That is why I have tried in the main to make this one complementary to, rather than a repetition of, topics in my previous publications. Indeed, it contains many facts that, to the best of my knowledge, have never appeared in ANY book before. Thus if you find a favourite old subject is not included, it will almost certainly be because it is already in one of my other works.

Of course, no history of Kingston could be written without the support of Kingston Museum and Heritage Service in the person of its head, Anne McCormack; the Borough Archivist, Jill Lamb; and the Local History Officer, Emma Rummins. For them the history of England's oldest Royal borough is not just a job, but also a deeply held interest.

This, together with their unfailing helpfulness, patience and good cheer, works wonders in motivating flagging authors and lightening the often onerous job of research.

Thanks are due to the *Surrey Comet*, Surrey's oldest surviving newspaper, and a long-time champion of local heritage, for allowing me to use many of its pictures.

I must also pay tribute to John Richardson, who requires his Historical Publications books to be factually accurate as well as interesting. Too many 'local history' publishers only demand the latter!

That is why, having vowed I would never write another book, I could not resist John's invitation to do this one.

All Saints Church

All Saints has been at the heart of Kingston since at least the 8th century, and seven Saxon kings are reputed to have been crowned there. Known until the Reformation as All Hallows, it was originally a minster serving a large area, including Richmond, Petersham, Ham, Hook, East Molesey and Thames Ditton, as well as Kingston.

The Saxon church was probably wrecked by Danish invaders, who in 1019 swept up the Thames as far as Staines, killing priests, and looting and burning churches as they went. In the 12th century it was rebuilt by the Sheriff of Surrey, Gilbert the Norman, who had been given the living by Henry I. Gilbert then gave it to Merton Priory, which he had founded with royal permission in 1117. The Priory retained it until Henry VIII's dissolution of monasteries in 1530. Now the patronage is held by King's College, Cambridge.

The Norman building was refurbished and enlarged in the 14th century. There have been many alterations since, notably an extensive re-modelling in the 19th century when, regrettably, some interesting old features were destroyed, including a Norman doorway.

The church has had an eventful past. The tower lost its wooden spire in 1445 to "a great weathering of wind, hayle, snow, rayne and thunder with lightening". It was rebuilt, only to be destroyed and never replaced after a "great Winde and Hurricane" in 1703. And during the 17th-century Civil Wars, troops looted the building, and used it as stables and lavatories.

2. *All Saints church in 1851.*

The tower was largely rebuilt in 1709, and again in 1973. But its 13th century base survives, and the original Norman chalk tower is thought to be encased intact within the present structure.

By 1997, the building was in such disrepair that a public appeal was launched to raise £2 million for restoration and modernisation. The work, and the appeal, is still in progress.

All Saints is one of the few parish churches to have a full cathedral peal of 12 bells, plus a carillon that plays four times daily. The original purpose of bells in a tower was "to give notice of death, to give notice of divine service by chiming and to give pleasure in times of public rejoicing." The earliest known written reference to the bells dates from 1503 when 2s 9d (about 17p) was "payd to Robert for oyle for a rope for the chyme" Thereafter they feature in church accounts down the ages.

3. *All Saints, c.1904.*

All Saints choir is noted as one of the finest parochial choirs in the UK while its superb Frobenius organ, installed in 1988, attracts the world's leading organists.

The Queen came to the church during her golden jubilee year to unveil a stone commemorating the crowning there of her predecessor, Edward the Elder, in 900.

After more than a thousand years as Kingston's only Anglican place of worship, the custom of referring to All Saints as Kingston Parish Church is ingrained, even though other parishes now share the Royal borough.

4. *The interior of All Saints Church, painted by T. Allom in 1840. During drastic alterations in the 1850s and 60s, the high boxed pews were removed, the plaster ceiling taken down to reveal the open timbered roof, and the organ gallery replaced by the fine west window. This depicts Christ in Majesty, with apostles modelled on local personalities of the time.*

Archaeology

Until the late 20th century, Kingston was largely ignored by professional historians because most of its past was hidden below ground for hundreds, even thousands of years. Not until the 1960s, with the start of site clearance for the restructuring of the town centre, could amateur volunteers, led by Kingston Museum, dig up some answers before developers moved in with deep-pile foundations.

A major find emerged in 1969 - still known in local history circles as 'jackpot year' - when volunteers unearthed part of a 600-year-old pottery kiln behind 70/72 Eden Street. This was highly significant discovery and inspired the establishment of Kingston upon Thames Archaeological Society (KUTAS) the following year. For, though the town was known to have supplied the highest people in the land, including the Royal court, with their cooking and tableware, it had been assumed these items were made elsewhere, with Kingston merely a trading channel. But the kiln discovery proved Kingston had been a key manufacturing centre as well as a trading one. It also led to a re-writing of specialist textbooks because more than half a ton of pottery was recovered from the site, all in an off-white composition with a green glaze. This had long been called Cheam Ware, because the only previously known medieval manufacture of it was at Cheam. But following the Kingston find, it was re-named Surrey Ware, with a separate subsection known to professionals

5. Four Iron Age gold coins of the early 1st century BC were discovered by metal detectors at Chessington in 1998. They were bought for Kingston Museum with funds from the V & A Purchase Grant Fund, the National Arts Collections Fund, the Friends of Kingston Museum and Heritage Service. Another two coins, discovered in Chessington in 1999, were also bought for the Museum, where all six coins are on display in the Ancient Origins Gallery.

6. Pottery from a 14th-century kiln excavated in Eden Street in 1995.

ever since as Kingston-type ware.

That was that for the next 27 years. Then, in 1995, the sites of 70/76 Eden Street were cleared for the building of a new C & A store. This time the volunteers were led by a professional team from the Museum of London Archaeology Service in a three-month dig funded by C & A. They not only unearthed the rest of the 1968 kiln, but found three more, all dating back to the 14th century. Now a reconstruction of one of the kilns as it would have looked in its heyday is on show at Kingston Museum, together with some fine examples of the Kingston Ware that was London's most fashionable pottery from about 1230. Henry III certainly liked it. State papers show that no fewer than 3,300 pitchers were ordered from Kingston for the Royal table between 1264/66.

The heavily urbanised Eden Street of today is largely given over to building societies, insurance companies and kindred white-collar activities. In medieval times it was a marshy waste on the outskirt of town, where potteries and other 'dirty' industries were concentrated. From here Kingston captured about a quarter of the London pottery market with its whiteware. Then the boom ended, and by about 1340 the kilns ceased production. Their superstructures were demolished, their chambers and stoking pits infilled, and they lay forgotten until their re-discovery more than six centuries later. *(See also Charter Quay)*

7. King Athelstan, as depicted on Maggie Humphrey's mural in Eden Street.

Athelstan

Athelstan was the first ruler to be recognised as King of All England and, but for his premature death, would doubtless have gone into history as one our finest. He was crowned King of Wessex and Mercia in Kingston in 924. An able and courageous soldier, he beat off many invaders, most notably at the Battle of Brunnanburh, where he conquered a combined invasion by the Danes, Scots, Welsh and Irish.

Off the battlefield he was an enlightened ruler who re-ordered the legal system, introduced currency control and strengthened international relations by negotiating the marriages of four of his half sisters to overseas rulers. He was also a cultivated man, and a connoisseur of the arts.

His death in 940, when he was only 44, and at the height of his power, was a huge setback to the united England he

8. Athelstan, a model using every known detail of his face and clothing. His figure greets visitors to 'Town of Kings' in Kingston Museum.

had striven so ably to achieve.

The millenary of his coronation in Kingston was commemorated in 1934 by the opening of Athelstan Bridge and Athelstan Recreation Ground, both in Villiers Road, and the unveiling of a stained glass window that is now in Kingston Museum. He is also remembered in the name of a school and a road; and a life-size model of him, based on contemporary descriptions of his appearance and dress, welcomes visitors to Kingston Museum.

Thomas Barnardo

On 19 September 1905 the blinds came down on the windows of St Leonard's Lodge in Portsmouth Road.

Thomas Barnardo (1845-1905), one of the most remarkable men of his age, had died. He is still a household name, though it is little known that he lived and died in the Royal borough. In fact, most of his final weeks were spent in an agonising time race across Europe so

9. Dr Thomas Barnardo – a Stepney portrait.

that he could die in his ugly, ivy-coated house near the Thames. The Barnardos had settled there in 1897, having combed London for their ideal home. The household consisted of the doctor, his wife Syrie, their daughter Queenie and nephew, George Barnardo.

For Dr Barnardo, an ailing man, the daily journey to his office in Stepney was exhausting. Often he spent the morning working at home, arriving at his office early in the afternoon, and working there until there was just time for his cabman to rush him to the last train. Once on board it was thanks to the stationmaster at Surbiton, who waited on the platform every night ready to lift him out of the train, that he did not travel well past his destination, sound asleep. When he got home at midnight he would find in his study a beef sandwich, held in a book press so the juices were absorbed by the bread - an idea he had evolved for himself. Fortified by this, he would work on papers brought from his office until 2.30am.

In 1902 the beautiful Queenie (later called Syrie after her mother) walked up the aisle of Christ Church, Surbiton for her ill-starred wedding to Henry Wellcome, American founder of the chemicals firm, Burroughs Wellcome. Her father bitterly opposed the match, but was abroad for medical treatment when it took place.

Syrie's second attempt at marriage was equally disastrous. In 1917 she married author Somerset Maugham and the intimacies, or lack of them, of their married life, provided much salacious Sunday newspaper reading in later years.

The house where Thomas Barnardo's wife said they spent the happiest years of their life together, is no more. In its place, on the corner of St Leonard's Road, is Ravensview Court, an apartment block with nothing externally to commemorate the exceptional man who lived there. This would pique him, for he always craved, but in his lifetime never achieved, official recognition of his accomplishments. By the time of his death he had rescued some 60,000 destitute children, sacrificing his health, and shortening his life, to the task he began in 1867.

It is small wonder he was a controversial figure. On the one hand he was a Christian philanthropist, who read no book but the Bible. On the other he was autocratic and flamboyant, with an insatiable hunger for praise. He also outraged his contemporaries by being radically ahead of his time. For example, he kept an 'ever open doors' policy", pledging that no destitute child would ever be turned away. His policy of accepting all such children, including illegitimate, black or those with disabilities, was unheard of at a time when all other charities operated restrictions on their intake. And it was not until the Children's Act of 1948 that local authorities became responsible for homeless children.

Barnardo regularly and controversially kidnapped children from parents who were violent or cruel in an era when parents had absolute rights over their offspring. For this he made 88 court appearance, and the resulting publicity led to a change of law in 1881 that put the welfare of children above the rights of the parent.

For years he was the sole fundraiser for his organisation, pioneering money-raising methods that are still in use. By the time of his death, he had raised what was then the staggering figure of £3 million, and was operating 96 homes caring for nearly 8,000 children.

Barnardo's - it has dropped the 'Dr' prefix - is now the UK's largest children's charity, responsible for 361 services and helping more than 100,000 children a year, though it closed its last children's home in 1981. It also tackles AIDS and child sexual abuse, and works with families in various ways, including fostering and adoption, disability and domestic violence.

(See also Dalziel of Wooler Home below)

Cyril Barton

There is a simple grave on the far side of Kingston's Bonner Hill Cemetery, marked by a white military stone, but hard to find without help from the cemetery staff. In the grave rests Pilot Officer Cyril Barton, the only Victoria Cross holder to be buried in Kingston. He was also the only Second World War Halifax bomber crew member to be honoured with the VC, which takes precedence over all other awards, decorations and honours within the British Commonwealth. Indeed, it has been conferred on only 51 airmen since its inception by Queen Victoria in 1856.

Cyril Barton, popularly known as Cy, lived in Elm Road, New Malden with his parents and five siblings. After leaving Beverley Boys' School, he became an apprentice at the Hawker Aircraft factory in Kingston, and attended classes at Kingston Technical College in the evenings. On Sundays he was a regular worshipper at St John's Church, New Malden. He enlisted with the RAF in 1941, when he was 19. Soon afterwards he was sent to America for a year's course of special instruction, returning late in 1942 to qualify and secure his wings. Then, in July 1943, he embarked on his first operational flight.

Before taking off he gave his brother Kenneth a letter for his mother in the event of his death. It began: "I hope you will never receive this, but I quite expect you will. I am expecting to do my first operational flight in a few days. I know what ops over Germany mean, and I have no illusions about it."

On 5 January, 1944 Cy received his commission as a pilot officer, and on March 26 he was promoted to flying officer. On March 31 he died at dawn, aged 22.

His Halifax was one of the aircraft that had taken off from RAF Burn in Yorkshire the previous night in Bomber Command's ill-starred raid on Nuremberg. No fewer than 96 aircraft were lost during the next few hours. For Cy, disaster struck when his Halifax was attacked by a German Junkers 88. Through brilliant piloting, he eventually shook off his attacker. But he had lost 400 gallons of fuel from two ruptured tanks. Furthermore, one engine, the radio and intercom systems and the rear turret were out of action. However, his worst shock was the discovery that, because of a Morse Code misunderstanding, half of the six-man crew had baled out. This left Cy without his wireless operator, navigator and bomber.

In such desperate circumstances, he could justifiably have baled out with his three remaining crewmen. Or he could have jettisoned his bomb load and abandoned the mission. Instead he did what he saw as his duty – he flew doggedly on to his target and released the bombs himself.

Then he turned for home. Despite strong headwinds and a broken propeller, and with no navigational aids, he somehow made it across the North Sea. Spying the Durham coastline below, he gave his customary thumbs-up sign to his companions. As he did so the fuel ran out, the engines died, and alone in the cockpit he fought to guide the engineless bomber. Suddenly a group of miners' cottages loomed through the dawn mist. He managed to clear them, but the manoeuvre took the last vestige of speed and control. The Halifax crashed into the yard of Ryhope Colliery and Cy was killed. But his three crewmen, whom he had ordered into crash positions by the main spar, survived without serious injury.

The only consolation for the Barton family was that, unlike so many lost airmen, Cy could at least be laid to rest in his home territory. After a funeral service at St John's Church, he was buried in Bonner Hill Cemetery on 6 April, 1944. Three months later he was posthumously awarded the Victoria Cross.

The citation read: "In gallantly completing his last mission, in the face of almost impossible odds, this officer displayed unsurpassed courage and devotion to duty."

Even more moving was the letter which the devoutly Christian young Cy had written for his mother in the event of his death, extracts from which were published in many national newspapers at the time.

> "Except for leaving you, I am quite prepared to die," he wrote. "I know I shall survive the judgement because I have trusted in Christ as my saviour. All that I am anxious about is that you and the rest of the family will come to know Him."

The borough of Malden and Coombe, as it was before merging with Kingston in 1965, was deeply proud of its young hero.

10. An architect's sketch of Kingston's first swimming baths, opened in Wood Street in 1897.

The council presented his parents with a framed testimonial, launched a trust fund to pay for the education of his five siblings and named Barton Green in his memory.

Bathing

Kingston's first designated swimming area opened in 1872 when, following complaints of nude bathing, the council took a seven-year lease on Steven's Ait, put up a canvas screen and called it "the bathing place". However, it was banned to women and girls, and the depth and current made it suitable only for strong swimmers.

This made personal hygiene even more difficult. Few houses had baths and, as Councillor Van de Pant pointed out in 1880, when the Steven's Ait lease had expired, the poor were given coal, soup and blankets "but no means of being cleanly". He added it was not only the poor who never bathed. "Every class is suffering from this omission, especially ladies, who aren't allowed to swim except under cover."

The council made a miserly £1,000 available and local engineer John Dixon *(qv)* used all his ingenuity to construct a swimming pool for this meagre sum. He described it as "a pontoon with a bath in the shape of a grating suspended in the middle, providing the facility of bathing in the top stratum of the river without stirring up the mud and sediment by treading on it." The grating could be raised or lowered to provide shallow bathing for women and children and deep water for men and boys.

Dixon designed the bath to be entered by steps from Kingston Bridge. The Thames Conservators objected, so it was towed up-river to Town End Wharf and officially opened in July 1882.

The *Surrey Comet* hoped the new facility would "promote habits of cleanliness among the lower orders of the people", adding that "the promoters claim that bathing establishments of this description are superior to shore baths, which although professedly filled every day, are often filthy and stinking holes, infinitely worse than the river." Then the Conservators objected again, demanding the bath be moved down-stream to a malodorous spot near the tannery. Kingston Council refused, whereupon the Conservators despatched a steamer and flotilla of small boats loaded with navvies to remove it by force.

They were confronted by an

army of civic dignitaries and workmen, armed with poles to drive the invaders away. There was a violent struggle in which blood was spilled and insults hurled. Finally a conservator aimed a hitcher at the deputy mayor, Alderman Frederick Gould, ripping his trousers from his legs. This stripping away of civic dignity was too much for the police who had been lying in wait in South Lane. They sprang to the rescue and the Conservators fled to their boats and made off, to the derisory cheers of the local population.

So the floating pool remained in situ, a boon alike to swimmers and the hitherto great unwashed. By 1890 it was so dilapidated that the council held a competition for the design of a cheap replacement; but the prizes were so small that there were only five entries.

The winners quoted £4,435 for a fine building, which the council eagerly accepted. Alas, before work could begin the designers realised the true cost would be £8,400, and they were angrily dismissed.

By 1894, when out of 6,127 houses in the town, 4,346 had no bath, the floating pool was unusable. After bitter dispute a replacement eventually opened in Wood Street in 1897 with a 90-foot pool and 24 slipper baths. They soon proved inadequate, as did the Coronation Baths erected in Denmark Road in 1936. These closed in 1980 and four years later were replaced by the Kingfisher Pool, adjacent to Kingston Museum.

Ian Bazalgette

New Malden has another VC hero of the air *(see Barton above)*, who also died in 1944. He was Squadron Leader Ian Bazalgette, who lived in Sycamore Grove, attended Rokeby School in Wimbledon and became a pilot officer in 1943.

He had completed many daring raids, and won the DFC, before taking the controls of a Lancaster bomber for a daylight raid on a key storage depot in France on August 4, 1944.

The plane was set alight by anti-aircraft fire, but Bazalgette pressed on and delivered all his bombs on target. Then an engine failed, the entire starboard mainplane went up in flames and he ordered his crew to bale out if they could. He remained at the controls to try to land the crippled craft and save his wounded bomb aimer and air gunner. Skilfully avoiding a village, he brought the aircraft safely down. But it then exploded, and he and his two comrades were killed.

His posthumous VC was received by his mother in December 1945. New Malden's Bazalgette Gardens is named in his memory

Bentalls

Kingston's pre-eminence as a shopping centre owes much to the initiative of the Bentall family. In 1867 Frank Bentall took on a struggling little drapery shop in Clarence Street. Within a year he had increased weekly takings from £70 to £200 and began a gradual expansion that eventually, under the dynamic leadership of his son, Leonard, made Bentalls the largest privately owned store in Europe until it went public in 1946.

Leonard, who pioneered car parking, restaurants, escalators and other previously locally unknown department store facilities, is often referred to as "the man who made Kingston." He died in 1942, and his life-size bronze likeness, sculpted by Sir William Reid Dick, stands near one of the store entrances as a memorial to his enterprise.

His two sons, Gerald and Rowan, and later his grandson, Edward, took the helm until 2001, when the Kingston store and its five branches were acquired by Fenwicks.

Bentall Centre

In December 1987 Edward Bentall, chairman of Bentalls and great-grandson of its founder, hoisted himself into the cab of a piling rig and literally levered Kingston into a new chapter of retailing history. For the huge iron pile he manoeuvred into the ground that day represented the first act of constructing the new Bentall

11. Bentalls' first shop in 1867.

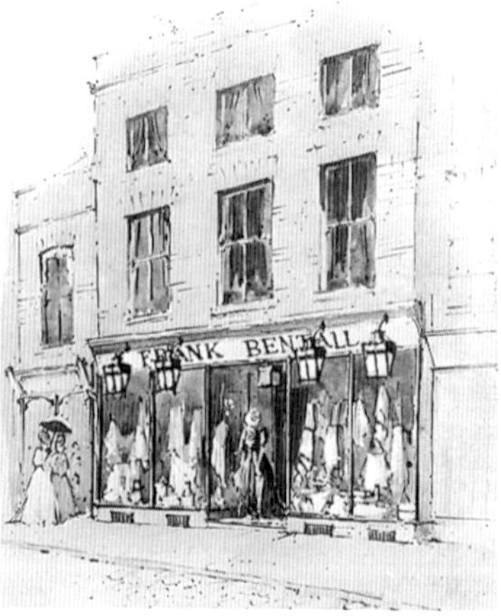

12. An artist's impression of the escalator hall which formed the centrepiece of Bentalls' Wood Street extensions, completed in 1935. It was demolished in 1990 to make way for the Bentall Centre.

13. *Wood Street in 1953. Bentalls store is on the right.*

14. *One of Bentalls' fleet of motor vans in 1929.*

15. A great engineering feat of 1990 was to retain Bentalls' famous façade and build the new Bentall Centre behind it. On the right is the Wood Street frontage of the John Lewis store, opened in 1990.

16. Wood Street, looking north, 1922. the vicarage on the right was acquired by Bentalls and its frontage incorporated in the store's façade.

department store that opened in July 1990 as Phase 1 of the Bentall Centre, a unique development by Bentalls in partnership with Norwich Union. Phase 2 of the project, said to be the biggest of its kind in Europe since the 1930s, opened in November 1992. Designed by Building Design Partnership on cathedral lines, it has four floors of shopping linked by 13 escalators and surmounted by one of the largest glass barrel-vaulted roofs ever constructed. The external walls retain the frontage that, modelled on the Sir Christopher Wren section of Hampton Court Palace, was a famous feature of the previous Bentalls store, which had occu-

17. The Bentall Centre.

18. The Bentall Centre's Clarence Street frontage.

pied the entire 3.5 acre site. Now the store, considerably more streamlined than its predecessor, stands at the northern end of the Bentall Centre, but operates independently from it.

Bishop's Hall

This lane, which links Thames Street with the riverside, is so named because the Bishops of Winchester had a mansion on its north side in the 13th and 14th centuries. By 1392 it had been leased to a layman, and Henry V is said to have been entertained there in 1414.

By 1664 the building had been replaced by a tannery, with the bishops' original cellars serving as tanning vats. The tannery was destroyed by fire in 1963. Now its site is covered by Bishop's Palace House – a complex of offices, shops, a restaurant and a nightclub adjacent to Kingston Bridge.

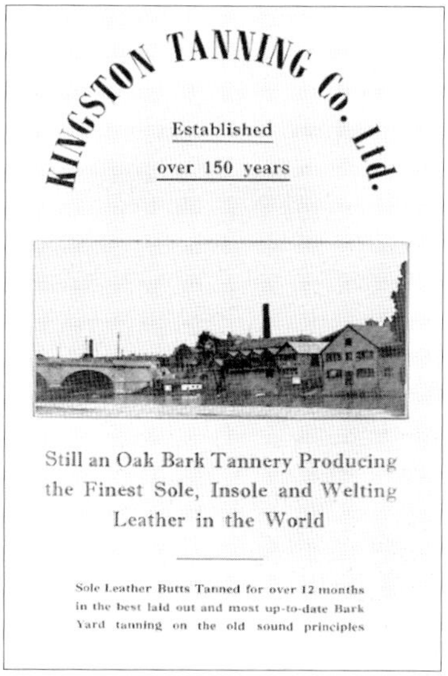

19. The Kingston Tannery at Bishop's Hall, from the Thames, c.1948.

On the south side of Bishop's Hall is The Bishop out of Residence, a public house built in 1980. Young's Brewery chose the name in the belief that if the bishops had remained in Kingston, they would have enjoyed this pub more than their palatial home!

Boatbuilding

During the 1880s a young man named Jerome Klapka Jerome discovered the joy of putting on a striped blazer, filling a hamper with goodies and taking the Sunday morning train to Kingston, accompanied by his friends, George Wingrave and Carl Hentschel. They would go to Turk's boatyard on Thames Side, hire a double sculling skiff (at a cost of £3.15s a week) and take to the river. The result, in 1889, was the publication of Jerome's comic classic, *Three Men in a Boat*. It is an account of a river cruise that began at Kingston and ended at Oxford, detailing all the ports of call, and intended as a tribute to the Thames at a time when it was providing Victorians with their greatest pleasure and recreation.

The book is still popular, and so is Turk's. Indeed, it is thought to be the oldest business of its kind in the UK to survive in the same family ownership, son succeeding father in an unbroken line.

The Turks had been involved in boat building for at least 700 years before Richard Turk set up his boatyard in Kingston in 1710. Evidently it prospered, for in 1777 George Constable and Samuel Slingsbury were commissioned to build a handsome new boathouse and workshop on the site.

Turk's still operate pleasure craft in Kingston, headed by Michael Turk, a direct descendant of the founder, but they no longer build boats there, concentrating instead on supplying craft to film-makers all over the world.

Michael's boats and the skills required to operate them, have been involved in well over a hundred top-class films, including *A Bridge Too Far, Shakespeare in Love, Elizabeth I,* several James Bond classics, and some of the Harry Potter films. But he now prefers to build his vessels overseas, where materials and labour are cheaper. One of his greatest creations is *Grand Turk*, a hand-crafted mahogany replica of a Napoleonic fighting ship. It took him four years to complete this 22-gun frigate, which he began building in the Turkish port of Marmaris to fulfil a boyhood dream. It was finished in 1997 as the first British-built ship of its kind for nearly 200 years, and played a starring role as *HMS Indefatigable* in Meridian TV's Hornblower series.

Another epic Turk achievement was a re-creation of the huge galleys used by the Greeks in their legendary ten-year war against Troy after Helen, the beautiful wife of King Menelaus was abducted by Paris, Prince of Troy. Legend has it that the Greeks launched a thousand fighting ships to rescue her. Michael, however, was asked to build only nine – later reduced to two – for Warner Brothers' blockbuster, *Troy*, released in 2004. Thanks to modern filming techniques the two vessels were made to look as if they numbered hundreds.

Part of the old Turk's workshop has been re-created at Kingston Museum, using original artefacts given by the family.

A few hundred yards upriver was Burgoine's boatbuilding works, established by brothers Charles and Alfred Burgoine in the 1860s. Alfred's design skills were a byword. His racing yachts were said to be second to none, as were his centre-board gigs. These included *Mona*, the first winner of the challenge cup presented by Queen Victoria to the Upper Thames Sailing Club in 1893, and *Ulva*, which twice won the Queen's Cup. In 1873 he received a Royal Appointment to build Queen Victoria's State Barge, rowed on the Thames by a crew of Queen's Watermen on many ceremonial occasions.

Burgoines later specialised in marine motoring, producing engines far ahead of their time. A major triumph was the *Maple Leaf*, which reached the

20. Michael Turk's galley for the film Troy, *pictured during shooting of the film in Malta.*

21. Two bright young things relax in a Burgoine boat in the 1920s.

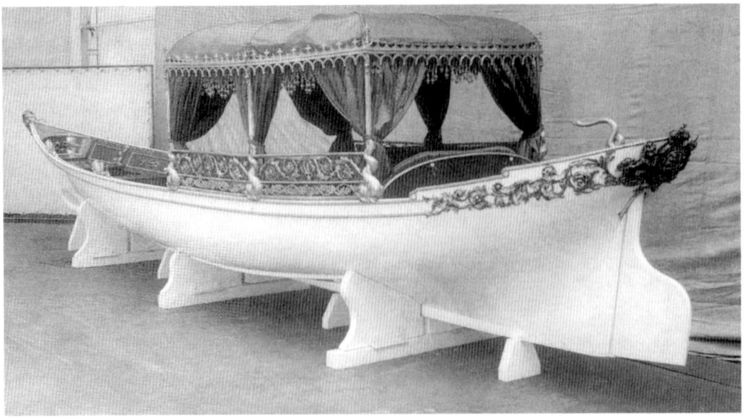

22. Queen Victoria's ceremonial barge built by Burgoine's of Kingston in 1873.

then astonishing speed of 65 mph.

Alfred's business acumen did not match his technical brilliance, and Burgoine's premises at 22 High Street, with a 150-foot river frontage, were sold in 1910. The company has long ceased to be a boat company and has evolved into the Offer Group, synonymous with building development and estate management. But its Hampton Wick site, redeveloped as offices, is still known as Burgoine Quay.

Benjamin Pope was a popular figure in Kingston's boating heyday. In 1880 he leased Picton House and its riverside grounds in High Street, and built and hired boats there until his death after the First World War. His best lines were houseboats and a special kind of skiff punt which he invented. All his craft were handmade from mahogany supplied by Gridley Miskin, a few hundred yards down-river.

The Eastlands were another Kingston boating family who lived and worked on Thames Side for nearly a century. They built skiffs and punts and hired them out. They left the river in 1958 and Len Eastland recalled when boating was such a competitive business that rival boatmen would go to Kingston Station touting for hire as day visitors got off the trains.

The Moulds had been on the river for more than a century when they finally retired in 1976. The firm was begun by William Mould, a chimney sweep who spent his spare time building a wooden steam launch on Kingston's public open space, The Fairfield. Equipped with this and another vessel he and his brother Tom set up a boat building and hiring business. They took on 39 High Street, a 17th-century building that is now a Pizza Express and established a boatyard at the back, living in the rooms above.

An unexpected chapter in Kingston's boat-building history came during the Second World War when W H Gaze and Son, long known as builders and garden designers, had to take on a new role of building boats for the Admiralty. They built more than 900 vessels, including 150 invasion craft that carried 7,500 men to the beaches of North Africa, Sicily and Normandy, plus 50 water ambulances and hundreds of naval assault craft. The vessels were made in improvised boatyards in High Street by men and women sworn to secrecy. Gaze's own specially designed trailers then took the boats to Town End Wharf, where they were launched into the Thames.

Bonner Hill School

This was a great landmark in the long history of local education, and there was an elaborate civic ceremony when it opened amid the former fields of Bonner Hill in March 1906. For this was the first school ever to be built by Kingston Corporation. Prior to that, all local schools had been established by the church, by private individuals or by charitable trusts.

The school, bounded by Bonner Hill Road and Villiers Road, was planned to accommodate 372 boys, 372 girls and 398 infants. The corporation organised an architectural competition to find the best design, finally selecting the entry by Mr F W Roper of London. Messrs Burges and Sons of Wimbledon constructed it at a cost of £15,687, and the result was a showpiece building, far ahead of its time.

Miss Annie Campbell, head of the infants' department, wrote an educational article for the *Surrey Comet* in 1908. Even today her views, as practised at Bonner Hill, sound startlingly *avant garde*.

23. *Bonner Hill school in 1908.*

"The subjects are not taught in isolation. The lines of division that usually mark off reading, writing and numbers simply do not exist," she wrote. "Reading, based on phonetics, writing, numbers, drawing is associated with the most varied forms of activity. Writing is learned incidentally, without any of the preliminary pot-hooks and elements of letters being needed. The command of the written forms gained in two or three weeks is at least equal to a year's copybook practice...in the various modes of free expression the artistic child, the imaginative child, the musical child, the child with a love of investigating, the child who enjoys constructing with his hands and the child who likes discovering reasons, has each a chance of exercising his own special talent..."

The school retained high standards throughout its 80-year existence. In its last years its thousand-plus mixed pupils were replaced by 400-plus girls. In the 1950s it was one of the first secondary schools in the country to sit for public examinations. In 1963 it was the first school in Surrey to instal dictating machines with multiple headphones for use in the commercial department, and as early as 1961 it had established a sixth form. It also reached county standard in sports, excelling in swimming and cross-country running.

The school closed in 1980. Three years later it was demolished, whereupond the two-acre site given over to housing.

Brewing

Brewing, together with its associated trades, was an important Kingston industry from the 16th to the late 20th centuries, originally with small independent brewers operating all over the borough. From the 18th century Rowlls Brewery began acquiring these little firms, and by the mid-19th century was well on its way to a monopoly of local brewing with extensive premises in Brook Street, adjoining the Rowlls family's splendid park and mansion.

In 1854 the brewery and its 90 tied pubs were acquired by William Hodgson, and by 1900 Hodgson's Kingston Brewery was one of Britain's major brewing concerns, with 130 tied houses. But Hodgson's still had its eyes on another big prize.

On May 11, 1903 the principal brewers of Britain assembled at the London Auction Mart hours before the appointed time. What had brought them together in the overcrowded room, while dozens more tried vainly to cram through the doors, was the sale of Fricker's Eagle Brewery in Kingston High Street and the 28 pubs that went with it. Bidding soared until there were only two contestants left: Hodgson's and Charrington's. Hodgson's eventually won with bids totalling more than £121,000.

Covetous eyes had been cast on Fricker's Eagle brewery and its fine river frontage since 1886, when Arthur Fricker died prematurely, directing that his firm be carried on by trustees during the minority of his children. Prodigious efforts were made by the trustees to retain possession and avoid sale. They even made applications to that effect to the Court of Chancery, but to no avail. The sale was forced through, and the name Fricker vanished from Eagle Wharf. The Eagle Brewery was continued by Hodgson's for a few years, but their main interest in the deal had been the Fricker pubs.

By the 1920s Eagle Wharf was given over to coal wharves, and today only the Eagle Tap, rebuilt by Hodgson's in 1915, and now home to a children's clothing boutique, survives as

24. *Fricker's Brewery on the Kingston riverside. This watercolour, painted by Charles Brindley in 1910, was bought for Kingston Museum by public subscription in 2002.*

25. *Victorian draymen line up outside the Kingston Brewery in Brook Street ready for the day's deliveries.*

26. *A rare picture of Hodgson's Brewery showing one of their early motorised vehicles.*

a physical reminder that here was once a brewery producing 7,500 barrels a year.

In 1943 Hodgson's Kingston Brewery was acquired by Courage but in 1951, because of the growing popularity of bottled beer, Courage ceased brewing there, and gave the premises over to bottling. The brewery closed in 1965 and it was here that Kingston's first major post-war commercial development was started in 1971. The scheme was carried out by the Sun Alliance and London Insurance group, which acquired the land from Courage. Its main component was a 100,000 square foot office block, earmarked by Lever Brothers as their head office before a brick had been laid. There was also a 40,000 square foot Tesco supermarket, a multi-storey car park, shops and a Courage pub on the Eden Street side. Tesco and the pub - the Seven Saxons - later closed and their sites are now occupied by a night club and shop respectively.

Though Fricker's Brewery has gone, many of its pubs remain. The most venerable of them is the Ram, which still stands alongside the former brewery entrance in High Street. Other survivors include the Albion, the Richmond Park Hotel, the Prince of Wales, the Artful Dodger (formerly the South Western Tavern) and the Crooked Billet at Ham.

Sir Sydney Camm

It was ironic that the centenary of Sydney Camm's birth coincided with the last stages of the demolition of the great British Aerospace works in Kingston. For, to the cognoscenti, it had been a huge public monument to him. Certainly it would not have been built but for him, and certainly it was because of him that Kingston remained a world-renowned centre of aircraft design and production for so long.

Camm, one of family of 12 children, was born in Windsor in 1894. He left school at 14 and began training as a carpenter like his father before him. In 1914 he joined the Martinsyde aircraft works at Brooklands, near Weybridge. But such was his skill and enthusiasm that during the First World War he was promoted from shop floor to drawing office in one exceptional leap.

His long career in Kingston began in 1923, when he became a senior designer and draughtsman at the H G Hawker Engineering Co. in Canbury Park Road, Kingston. Here his first professional design was the Hawker Cygnet, a light aircraft weighing only 375lbs. In 1925 he became Hawker's chief designer, a post he retained until becoming chief engineer 34 years later. Under him, the Hawker design team developed the technical skills that won a steady stream of contracts, and enabled Sopwith's small firm to develop into the mighty Hawker Siddeley Aircraft Co. His most notable achievement was the development of the Hurricane airplane, which was to play such an important part in the Second World War. Its first flight was in 1935 and it was the first fighter plane to break the 300mph barrier - 600 of these were ordered by the RAF.

Camm began revolutionising production to cope with the huge demand for aircraft in the wae. He was a hard task-master. "He never, ever, had praise for what you had done, rarely so much as an encouraging word" one of his subordinates recalled. "It was an iron discipline that ensured you had done your very best before you laid out your work before him."

Another remembered Camm's ability "to give an instant and bowel-churning dressing down", and the fact that he would "brook no irreverence or argument from his men." Tom Sopwith himself described him as "impossible"

27. 'Tom' Sopwith.

and said he could not imagine why Camm's men had put up with him. Dr John Fozard, who worked under Camm for 16 years, related in his book, *Sydney Camm and the Hurricane,* that some 27,000 high performance military aircraft were built to Camm's designs over 65 years, plus about 50 aircraft types.

"His first decade at Kingston laid the foundations for what became an awesome industrial empire," wrote Dr Fozard. "He hired, trained and nourished professionally many men whose career and contribution is now recognised internationally. Most important of all, Camm with his small team of the mid-1930s, working in shabby premises in a run-down Kingston back street, changed the course of history and thus preserved our way of life and our civilisation."

Though Camm was such a martinet at work, he was basically a shy man, who shunned publicity and, always mindful of his humble origins, seemed surprised when he was sought out by people of position and influence. He was even more surprised, and touchingly proud, when he was made a CBE in 1941, knighted in 1953 and awarded the Royal Aeronautical Society's gold medal – its highest honour – in 1958.

His death at 72 came unexpectedly while playing golf on March 12, 1966. He had been working in the design office right up to the previous evening, and had lived long enough to see the company into its first monoplane, its first jet and finally into V/STOL (Vertical/Short Take-off and Landing) aircraft.

Camm's death certificate describes him simply as "aircraft designer kt, CBE." It is strictly accurate and to the point. Just as he was.

Canbury

This area of North Kingston, originally the manor of Canonbury, derives its name from the Augustinian canons of Merton Priory, who owned it from 1117 until 1538, when their great monastery near the River Wandle at Merton was dissolved by Henry VIII. All its possessions were then seized by the Crown and given to laymen. Thus the Hardinge family became Lords of the Manor of Canbury for more than a century. Later the manor was acquired by the Tollemache family of Ham House.

Until the mid-19th century, Canbury was a rural area of farms, orchards and market gardens. But it rapidly gave way to housing, shops and pubs after the opening of Kingston Station in 1863. The station was built on the site of a huge tithe barn – said to be the largest in Britain – that was used for the threshing and storage of grain grown in the manorial fields.

Canbury Gardens

Canbury Gardens was the inspiration of Samuel Gray, whose family had been maltsters and lightermen in Kingston since the 18th century. Gray was a founder of Canbury Ratepayers' Association, established early in the 1880s to give this developing and somewhat despised part of the town a voice.

He remembered the Canbury riverside in pre-railway days, when it was an isolated stretch of swamps and osier beds, teeming with snipe and kingfishers. After the arrival of the railway, and its attendant building expansion in the 1860s, the site became a tar manufactory and foul rubbish dump before, thanks to Gray, being transformed into the gardens that did so much to raise the attraction – and rateable values – of Canbury.

In 1884 Gray called a meeting to propose that the site be laid out as a public garden. Later that year he was elected councillor for Canbury Ward, and in 1887 proposed that the "tar paving manufactory, road materials and other unsavoury objects" be removed and that "the view from the river shall be a pleasant one and not, as at present, unsightly and obnoxious." The motion was defeated on the grounds that, if such a garden was created, "it would be used by working men."

But eventually plans were drawn up by the borough surveyor, Henry Macaulay, and the first section, extending 1,000 feet from the new Down Hall Road to a point in line with Kings Road, was completed in 1890 at a cost of £404.

28. The opening of Canbury Gardens on 8 November 1890, and below (29), a scene in the Gardens c.1904.

Extensions, plus turfing and landscaping, continued for the rest of the century, and it has remained one of Kingston's major scenic attractions ever since. In recent years the Victorian bandstand, removed in the 1950s as unsafe, has been replaced and concerts are again a feature.

Charter Quay

This is a modern name, conceived by Prudential Assurance in 1988 for the land it had just acquired for development on the west side of Kingston Market Place. The site backs on to the Thames, and its principal building had long been Hide's department store.

After submitting various schemes, Prudential eventually pulled out. In 1998 St George took over the derelict site and, before embarking on re-development, funded the most extensive archaeological excavations ever carried out in the town.

It was already known that Kingston had been a Saxon royal estate and administration centre, occupying a gravel island bounded by the Thames, the Hogsmill and other channels to the east and north. But when did it develop into an important inland port and market? The Charter Quay dig by Wessex Archaeology revealed that the island of Kingston was planned as a 'new town' in about 1170. The Market Place was laid out south of an existing settlement around All Saints church, four bridges were built to cross the Thames (Kingston Bridge), the Hogsmill (Clattern Bridge), the Downhall Ditch (Barre Bridge) and an eastern arm of the Hogsmill (Stone Bridge).

Kingston Bridge was rebuilt in the 1820s. Clattern Bridge survives, albeit widened and strengthened, and is a scheduled ancient monument. The other two have long since vanished

Another key find was several house timbers dating from the 12th century. This was particularly important because there are few remains of 12th-century timber buildings anywhere in Britain. The archaeologists found that by 1200 the Market Place frontage of Charter Quay was fully occupied by houses, possibly with shops and workshops at street level. Later one of these buildings had been dismantled and its oak timbers used to build a riverside revetment. The waterlogged conditions at the edge of the river ensured the timber's survival, and provided valuable help in deducing how some of the earliest buildings on the site were constructed.

30. The 19th-century footbridge that spanned the Hogsmill stream in Oil Mill Lane – later renamed Villiers Road. In the background is the oil mill.

Early documents list some of the traders who operated in the Charter Quay area, and their names give a clue to their occupations. For instance, there is le Coliere (charcoal supplier) and Orfevre (goldsmith). There is also Poter (potter) which tallies with the fact that medieval Kingston had a thriving pottery industry, and supplied the Royal court with thousands of pitchers.

Clattern Bridge originally marked the southern limit of the town. But in the 12th century the land between the bridge and Emms Passage developed into a small suburb of houses and yards called Claterinbrugende. The roadway south of the bridge was called Westbitamstrete, later West-by-Thames Street, and now High Street.

The Thames was formerly several yards wider than now and, as the town developed apace in the 14th and 15th centuries, there were constant efforts to reclaim land from the river by building revetments, or ramparts. These also served as flood defences and wharves for boats to load and unload.

After centuries as a centre for wharving, brewing, inn-keeping, tanning, candlemaking and other activities, the area had been largely given over to fashionable shops and a bank by the late 19th century. Then, as commercial activity gradually moved away from the waterfront after the 1950s, it went into decline, and by the 1980s had become largely derelict. It remained that way for the next 10 years as planning applications came and went. In 2003 St George completed their development of Charter Quay as apartments, houses, cafés, a riverside walk and the shell of a theatre, thus restoring vitality to this long neglected part of the town.

Cinemas

In the early 1950s, Kingston had five town centre cinemas: the Elite, the Granada, Kingston Kinema, the Regal and the Odeon. By 2002 all had closed.

The first to go was the Elite. A strikingly beautiful building, designed by Adamson and

31. Clattern Bridge in 1934 just before the Hogsmill was culverted.

Kinns to seat 1,237, it opened in 1921, and boasted an orchestra pit, an organ, a foyer lined with panelling and carved oak from a Kentish mansion, four tea-rooms and a coffee bar. In 1946 it was taken over by Granada Theatres and re-named Century Elite. In 1955 it was closed and demolished to make way for a C & A store.

The Odeon opened in Kingston High Street in 1933 and Oscar Deutsch intended it should be the first in his planned new Odeon circuit (named possibly after the Greek "Odeion" used for places of musical entertainment). To his chagrin, the work was so delayed by legal problems that Weymouth Odeon opened first. The Kingston one opened a month later, and Deutsch was there for the ceremony, along with Jack Buchanan, one of the great British stars of the 1930s.

Designed by architects J E Adamson, Marshall & Tweedy, it seated 1,516 and had a stage, two dressing rooms, an organ and was the only Odeon, apart from the one in London's Leicester Square, to have an orchestra pit with a lift.

The cinema closed in 1967 and was converted into a bingo hall. This too closed in 1987 and the building was demolished in 1989. The Rose of Kingston Theatre was built on the site in 2003.

The Regal was designed in 1930 by Robert Cromie and opened on the corner of the Richmond and Canbury Park Roads in 1932 to replace the Cinem Palace, which had opened on the site in 1909 as Kingston's first purpose-built cinema. The Regal had 2,433 seats plus full stage facilities, a fine Wurlitzer organ (with the famous Reginald Foort as resident organist) and a café with a sprung floor for tea dances.

In 1936 it was acquired by Union Cinemas and re-named the Union. The following year it was taken over by Associated British Cinemas and named the ABC, reverting to Regal in 1939. It became the ABC again in 1960. In 1976 it closed and the building, which was listed by the Department of the Environment in 1993, has been a bingo hall ever since. Meanwhile the café became Kingston Dance

32. Kingston Odeon in the 1950s.

Studio in 1959, and still remains so.

Kingston Kinema began life in 1910 as Kingston Picture Theatre. Designed by Walter Phillips for Surrey and Sussex Picture Palaces Ltd of Kingston Hill, it had 350 seats, and was noted as the first to serve free tea and biscuits at matinees. In 1930 the building - which stood on the corner of Clarence Street and Cromwell Road - was modernised with a new projection room and equipment, and the addition of a circle auditorium. In 1970 it closed for two weeks, re-opening as Studio 7, owned by Star Cinemas. After a spell as Studio X, showing uncensored films, it closed in 1983 and became a pine furniture shop until its demolition in 2000 to make way for the Rotunda leisure complex.

The Granada was designed by George Coles and opened in 1939 with 1,758 seats. Cinemascope with stereoscopic sound was added in 1954 and the addition of backstage dressing rooms in the 1960s made it a venue for pop concerts by the top stars of the day. It was converted to three screens in 1973.

It was Kingston's sole surviving cinema when it closed in February 1987, and work began the next day on converting it into a new complex housing three cinemas, a night club, restaurant and a coffee bar. But the conversion came to a dramatic halt when the Department of the Environment - alerted by the Cinema Theatre Association - intervened with a spot listing to preserve the original architecture of the

33. Bentalls' former furniture depository in Cromwell Road dates from 1936. A listed building, it now contains the largest Odeon cinema ever built.

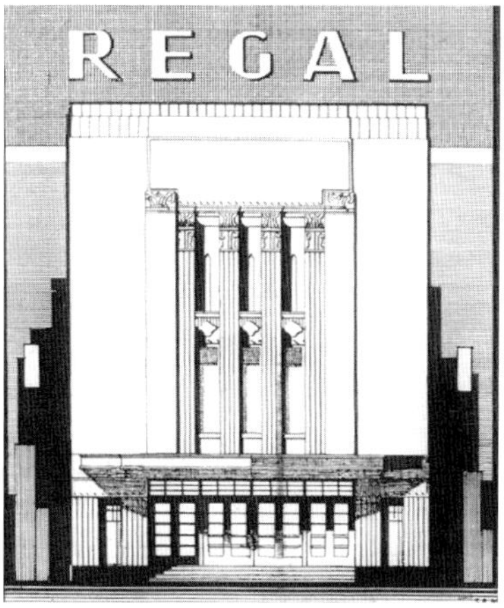

34. Architect's drawing for the Regal Cinema.

35. Clarence Street c.1906, looking east from Kingston Bridge. The churchyard railings are on the right.

36. Clarence Street after it was altered beyond recognition in the 1980s. The view shows the award-winning, but highly controversial John Lewis building, which has part of the relief road running through it. The two parts of the store are linked by an internal bridge.

building, which was said to one of the best of the 18 cinemas built by Granada during the 1930s, and the finest of the six still surviving at that time.

The club (Options) and the three-screen cinema became a reality later that year, but housed in a building that retained the beautiful foyer, staircase and the Komisarjevesky interiors.

In 2002 the cinema closed and the whole building was given over to the Oceana night club - but still preserving the best features of the original Granada.

That same year the largest Odeon Cinema ever built opened next door in the Rotunda complex.

Clarence Street

This thoroughfare, formerly Norbiton Street, existed some 800 years ago as the main route into the town from London. Its semi-rural atmosphere, and preponderance of ancient cottages, ended in the 1820s with the building of a new Kingston Bridge 50 yards upstream from the old. Norbiton Street was extended to form a direct approach to the new structure, and re-named Clarence Street in honour of the Duchess of Clarence (later Queen Adelaide) who opened the bridge in 1828.

After that it gradually gained its present status as Kingston's main shopping street. But traffic en-route to the all-important bridge was a mounting problem until, following the construction of a relief road around the town, the major part of the street was pedestrianised in 1989.

Cleave's Almshouses

The almshouses were established by the will of William Cleave in 1665, which left money "for the erecting and building of a convenient house" for "six poor men and six poor women of honest life and reputation". They were built in 1669, extended in 1889, and substantially refurbished and modernised in 1994. They survive to this day in London Road, administered by Kingston United Charities, set up in 1931.

37. *Cleave's almshouses.*

Coronation Stone

There is an ancient tradition that seven Saxon kings were crowned in Kingston, though there is firm documentary evidence for only two. The sandstone slab on which they are said to have sat during their coronations is preserved alongside the Guildhall.

This stone is thought to have lain originally in St Mary's Chapel, the Saxon building that stood to the south of Kingston parish church until it collapsed in 1730 after being undermined by the grave-digging exertions of the sexton, Abram Hammerton, and his son and daughter. Abram was killed, and his children buried for more than seven hours before rescuers could dig them free. The daughter, Esther, then succeeded her father as sexton, and has gone into local history as a minor celebrity!

The stone was then moved to the Market Place and used as a mounting block. In 1850 it was 're-discovered', encircled by Saxon-style pillars and railings, and formally inaugurated as a monument on September 19th during a day of rejoicing in which the whole town took part.

The seven coronations traditionally believed to have taken place in Kingston are those of Edward the Elder, son of Alfred the Great, in 900; Athelstan in 925; Edmund in 940; Edred in 946; Edwy in 956; Edward the Martyr in 975 and Ethelred the Unready in 979.

There is strong documentary evidence for Athelstan and Ethelred, but the claims for the other five are less convincing. However, in a charter of 946 King Edred refers to Kingston as the place "where coronations are accustomed to be held."

It is popularly, but erroneously, believed that Kingston

39. *Esther Hammerton, the Kingston sexton.*

38. *A ticket to celebrate moving the Coronation Stone in 1850.*

40. The Coronation Stone in the 1880s. Market Place is in the background.

41. St Mary's Chapel.

derives its name from the "King's stone" i.e the Coronation Stone. In fact it comes from Cyningestun, or King's Tun, meaning a royal estate.

Crimes and Punishments

By the eighteenth century, according to William Biden, "every vice and every species of immorality was practised more or less openly" in Kingston, and in 1773 Parliament passed an Act for the Lighting and Watching of Kingston. This authorised the corporation to appoint up to fourteen paid watchmen, who could be armed at night. The number actually appointed was far fewer and they were always a motley crew.

In 1897 Philip Jones recalled them seventy years earlier. "They gathered at 10pm when the curfew bell was rung, and they would sing out 'past ten o'clock and a moonlight night', and then hurry off to find the nearest drinking place. There used to be watchboxes at various corners, and some rare fun we used to have with the old Charlies... as they used to frequently sleep while on duty. It was a standing joke for the young sparks to turn over the watchbox with the Charlie inside it." One Charlie had a wooden leg. Another was so old and small that as he shuffled along the lantern dragged the ground.

In 1835 the Borough Police Act compelled Kingston to set up a Watch Committee and reorganise the watching system on the lines of the Metropolitan Police. Five paid constables were appointed "making the whole number with those at present on the watch nine constables". Day constables were to be paid a weekly 18s, night watchmen 14s, and "cloathed in an uniform manner, with blue coats, waistcoats, trousers, glazed hats, oil skin capes and great coats... the night constables to carry for their protection, and those of the inhabitants, a cutlass, rattle, dark lanthorn,

42. The Coronation Stone was moved to its present position beside the Hogsmill stream after completion of the new Guildhall (seen in the background) in 1935.

43. *The Debtors' Prison at the Hand and Mace. It was pulled down in 1831.*

and a staff... they should go their rounds silently and without calling the hour."

Their headquarters were under the old town hall, and the watch-house, built in Union Street in 1825, continued as the chief rallying point for the night watch.

Fearful that the Metropolitan Police would take over responsibility for policing the area, the council provided a new police station near Clattern Bridge. To no avail, for in 1839 Kingston was brought into the Metropolitan Police district and the new police station, as well as their chief constable, were declined.

A new police station was built in London Road in 1864 and it remained the police HQ until 1968, when new premises were built by the Guildhall.

Early punishments could be placement in the stocks or pillory, or public whipping in the Market Place. Public burnings were also held there, while hanging usually took place on a stretch of open land at the top of Kingston Hill. The parish register for 8 September, 1572, records: "This day in this towne... was hangid six persons and seventeen taken for roges and vagabonds and whippid abowte the market place and brent in the ears".

During the eighteenth and nineteenth centuries the Assize

44. *Kingston police force in 1888.*

records show many hangings and transportations. Mary Langsden was hanged in 1753 for stealing a purse. Charles Manmore was sentended to death in 1833 for stealing a horse, and Samuel Rose was transported for seven years for stealing a ring.

The most remarkable sentencing occurred in 1795, when the *European Magazine* records what happened in Kingston: "One Gregory was hanged for horse stealing, and at the same time no less than 11 of his own sons were hung by his side on the same gallows for repeated crimes of the same nature; and what is yet more singular, one Colman, with his five sons, were hung on the same gallows at the same moment in all 18 in number."

'Bad-tempered' women, usually called 'scolds' were ducked as a punishment. They were put in a ducking stool, a chair which hung from an axle attached to the end of two long poles. The whole contraption was mounted on three wheels so the victim could be tied to the seat and wheeled publicly through the town to Kingston Bridge. The parish records of 1572 record one poor woman being ducked 111 times on the same occasion.

Use of the ducking stool had ceased by the nineteenth century, but for some years scolds were publicly humiliated by having the old stool propped up outside their homes.

Kingston had two prisons, both grim. One was the debtors' gaol, built in 1505, and run by local victuallers who were permitted to operate an alehouse on the premises in lieu of salary. Conditions for prisoners were very hard, with the management supplying a minimum of water and food, but no bedding. This prison was pulled down in 1831 for widening of the road to the new Kingston Bridge.

Kingston also had Surrey County Gaol, opened in 1761 off what is now Lady Booth Road. The *Gentleman's Magazine* in 1804 reported that prisoners had scanty rations, allowed one pound of bread each per day with only water to drink. The county allowed nothing but straw to lie on.

This House of Correction was closed in 1852 after the opening of the new county

45. Aerial view of a Dr Barnardo's – the Dalziel of Wooler Home (see facing page). In the background is part of Coombe Wood golf course and Coombe Wood tennis courts. In the foreground is Galsworthy Road. Blenheim Gardens was built on this site in the 1960s.

prison at Wandsworth. The building then became a temporary barracks for the 3rd Surrey Militia until 1875.

Dalziel of Wooler Home

A Dr Barnardo's Home *(see Dr Barnardo above)* was a familiar landmark on Kingston Hill until 1968. Named the Dalziel of Wooler Home, in honour of the donor, it was a distinctive, neo-medieval building that was originally opened in 1875 as the Metropolitan Convalescent Institution, offering free accommodation to poor children recovering from serious illness, and promising "a plentiful, wholesome diet, fresh air and country scenes" at a time when Kingston Hill was indeed rural.

In 1892 the building was bought by the National Society for the Protection of Young Girls, and opened by Princess Louise as a home "to save young girls between the ages of 11 and 15, from any part of the kingdom, whether orphans or otherwise, who are from any circumstances exposed to temptation or in danger of being abandoned..."

The Princess Louise Home, as it became known, closed through lack of funds in 1933. The building was then bought and re-fitted by Lady Dalziel of Wooler, and presented to Dr Barnardo's as a home for 150 boys. It closed in 1968. Soon afterwards it was demolished and replaced by the houses of Blenheim Gardens.

Charles Dickens

Charles Dickens never lived in Kingston, but he was a frequent visitor. George Ayliffe recalls in his *Memories of An Octogenarian* that the great author used to stay at The Wheatsheaf, an old hostelry on the east side of Kingston Market Place. The pub closed in the 1960s and the building - what is left of it - is now a branch of Rymans.

Dickens was evidently impressed by the Kingston Hill area, for he used it as a setting in *Master Humphrey's Clock*, a miscellany in which Mr Pickwick re-appears, and tells a story about the witches and the gibbet on Kingston Hill that had the civic dignitaries listening spellbound in Kingston Town Hall. It gives a vivid picture of the hill between the Ladderstile and what is now the Kingston Lodge Hotel when it was a desolate, windy heath, silent save for the clank of the chains against the gibbet.

46. Charles Dickens, a photograph taken by Claudet in 1852.

John Dixon

John Dixon was an intriguing personality who combined the precision of an engineer with the optimism of a born gambler. Had he not been, Britain might never have acquired Cleopatra's Needle, the well-known landmark on the Embankment in London.

Though born in Liverpool, Dixon made Kingston his home. He settled in a house overlooking the Thames in Portsmouth Road, and from there embarked on some great professional adventures, including the design and construction of China's first railway in 1876. But his most audacious engineering feat began in 1877, when he took up a challenge that had defeated the best brains in Britain for decades: the moving of the so-called Cleopatra's Needle from the hot sands of Alexandria to the chilly banks of the Thames in London.

The Needle is an Egyptian obelisk, carved from a single hunk of pink granite 18 centuries before the birth of Christ. Originally it had been one of a pair erected in front of the Great Temple of the Sun in what is now Cairo to commemorate the victories of Pharoah Thothmes III. It got its name because Cleopatra is reputed to have had both obelisks transferred to her palace at Alexandria. There they were discovered by Napoleon when he invaded Egypt in 1798. He found one still standing, the other half buried in sand, and would have taken both back to France had he not been defeated by Nelson at the Battle of the Nile.

The Earl of Cavan, commander of the British troops in Egypt, wanted to celebrate the victory by transporting one of the obelisks back to Britain. His troops agreed, and gave £7,000 to finance the scheme. But the military authorities in London were not interested, and the cash was refunded.

However, the idea had fired the imagination of engineers, who racked their brains as to how it could be fulfilled. Their efforts redoubled in 1820, when Mehemet Ali, the Viceroy of Egypt, formally offered the recumbent obelisk to Britain to mark the accession of George !V. Again, nothing happened.

It was Britain's long-standing rivalry with France that really got things moving when the French then triumphantly brought an obelisk from Luxor and erected it in the Place de La Concorde in Paris. Amid the jealous controversy that followed, Prince Albert suggested that Britain could outdo France by bringing Cleopatra's Needle to London. Inventor after inventor came up with schemes. None was feasible.

Finally, in 1877, a London surgeon named Erasmus Wilson offered £10,000 towards the costs. John Dixon, his gambler's instinct roused, took on the task. His terms were simple. If he succeeded where so many others had failed, he would receive a large slice of the cash. If he failed, even after months of work, he would get nothing.

It was an immense task. The Needle was 70 foot long and weighed some 200 tons. To add to the problem it lay in sand 15 feet above the high water line on the Alexandrian coast. Dixion's plan was ingenious. He would encase the Needle in a cylindrical iron vessel. The entire mass, weighing nearly 300 tons, would then be towed through the Mediterranean and up the Atlantic to England.

By spring 1877 the Needle's giant wrappings were being made in the Thames Iron Works before being shipped out to Alexandria in sections. John Dixon enlisted the aid of his brother, Wayneman, in directing the task of literally wrapping the Needle up into a huge waterproof parcel. First they had to scoop out hundreds of tons of sand from around the fallen giant. Then it had to be heaved up on powerful jacks specially brought from Britain. Finally the parcelling work could begin.

After three months' labour, the Needle was safely secured and ballasted into a vessel 92 feet long and 15 feet wide. It had a deckhouse, steering wheel and accommodation for three crew, and was affectionately christened *Cleopatra* by her creator.

The *Cleopatra* had been designed to float in a mere nine feet of water, but to reach that depth it had to be rolled 400 feet. On 28 August, 1877 this tricky operation took place and Dixon heaved a sigh of relief as the vessel successfully reached the water. But his happiness was short-lived. A rock pierced the iron plating.

The vessel was pumped dry and repaired. On September 21 the English steamship *Olga* sailed out of Alexandra with the *Cleopatra* in tow, and reached the Bay of Biscay without incident. Then a fierce storm shifted *Cleopatra's* ballast, and the *Olga's* captain decided to evacuate her crew and cut the 400 yards of steel towing cable. The result was tragedy. Six of the *Olga's* men died in the first abortive attempt to get a boat alongside the lurching *Cleopatra* and take off her crew. The second try was successful, but two more of the *Olga's* crew were injured.

The *Cleopatra* was left to her fate; but Dixon's superb craftsmanship proved itself. After the storm, a passing steamer came across the vessel, drifting but intact, and towed her to the Spanish port of Valencia. The steamship's owner then claimed £5,000 salvage.

But Dixon was not to be beaten. He persuaded the Port of London to send its largest tug to bring *Cleopatra* home, and on 21 January, 1878 the battered maiden was triumphantly moored off Gravesend. After heated debate, it was decided to place it on the Embankment – a complex exercise that took weeks.

At last, on 12 September, John Dixon could savour his ultimate triumph by lowering Cleopatra's Needle on the site it has occupied ever since. But he got scant praise back home in Kingston.

"If this and larger monuments could be safely moved about some 1,500 years BC, it is not possible to to doubt our ability to do likewise in the 19th century AD" said the *Surrey Comet* dismissively.

Dixon's main claim to local fame was capaigning for, and designing, Kingston's first purpose-built swimming bath *(see under Bathing).*

Dixon's house is one of the few large Victorian villas still surviving in Portsmouth Road, though its name has been changed from The Choumbra to Anglesea Lodge, and it has been converted into flats.

John Eccles

Though the name John Eccles (1668-1735) is little known today, he was a great celebrity in the 17th and 18th centuries, and made a unique contribution to English music. He was the first composer, rather than performance musician, to occupy the post of Master of the King's Musick from 1700, which he held through four reigns (William II, Queen Anne, George I and George II). And he was the first composer to write an English opera in the so-called Italian style, which became the basis of opera as we know it today.

He was born possibly in or near Kingston, and was the eldest son of Solomon Eccles, a professional musician until he converted to Quakerism, burned all his music and instruments and took up cobbling. Solomon became a noted religious fanatic, parading the streets of London naked but for a loin cloth, with a burning brazier balanced on his head. When his religious passions cooled he took up music again, and taught John the violin.

John's early life is obscure, but around 1690 he began composing for the theatre, which was then on a pinnacle of fashion and popularity. He became musical director of the new theatre at Lincoln's Inn Fields and poured out music for 55 plays, of which the best remembered are Congreve's *Love for Love* and *The Way of the World* and Vanbrugh's *The Provoked Wife*. Indeed, his works were the pop music of their day, and when a hundred of his tunes were published as a collection in 1710 it sold so well that a second collection was hurriedly brought out.

Italian opera came to London early in the 18th century, and was so successful that Eccles and Congreve decided to write what they described as "the first all-sung English opera." The result was *Semele*, completed in 1709 but, for some reason, rejected for public performance.

Eccles was so discouraged that he retired to Kingston, and spent the last 25 years of his life in a house on the west side of Kingston Market Place. It stood roughly where NatWest is now, and its riverside garden enabled him to indulge his passion for fishing.

However, he retained his position and annual salary of £200 as Master of the Royal Musick. When he moved to Kingston he stopped composing for Queen Anne's Court; but after her death in 1735 he composed the Birthday and New Year Odes every year until he died. The only times he stirred from Kingston was on these two annual occasions, when he went to London to rehearse and perform the music for George I and George II.

Eden Street

Until Victorian times, Eden Street was called Heathen Street. A deed in the borough archives, which describes it as Hethenstrate, shows that that had been its name since at least 1315, and it worried no-one until a prosperous auctioneer called John Dawson came to live there. He was not only one of the most influential men in the town (there is a road named after him), but also a leader of the Independent chapel near his house. Thus he was embarrassed at having to give both his house and church address as Heathen Street.

Once he began agitating, people realised it was rather comical that a street so full of pious Christian denominations should bear such a pagan name. For, besides the Independents, the Quakers also had their meeting house there and the Methodists were preparing to build a church.

For centuries there had been bitterness between the Church of England body in the town and the non-conformists. The Anglicans saw the Heathen Street controversy as a heaven-sent chance to ridicule their rivals, and soon the Heathen Street worshippers were the butt of bad jokes all over the town. However, the ribald laughter brought matters to a head, and the council decided to let Mr Dawson have his way. The name Heathen Street was dropped and replaced by Mr Dawson's own choice, Eden Street.

But how did this ancient street come to be "heathen" in the first place? Archaeological excavations in the 1970s revealed that a tributary of the Thames had once flowed here. As the watercourse slowly dried up it became marsh and wasteland, with the road providing a more solid bank around the mud. It was a desolate country outpost, occupied by poor rustics and 'dirty' trades, such as pottery making

Two views of Eden Street c.1907. The top one (47) is looking north, when it was still a high class residential street. Now it is totally commercial with building societies, offices, shops etc. Below (48) is a view south from Clarence Street. In the distance is the spire of Kingston Methodist church, demolished in 1964.

and skinning. Like 'pagan' (meaning country man), 'Heathen' once had rustic associations, and both acquired their modern sense because country people tended to cling to their ancient superstitions while Christianity was developing in the towns.

Eden Walk Shopping Centre

It took 54 years to make Eden Walk a completed reality. The scheme was conceived in 1936, when Kingston Council was one of the first local authorities in Britain to recognise the long-term need for a multi-storey car park. Originally the complex was to be built on the Horsefair, and the basement of the car park was actually constructed there. Then came the Second World War and the basement became a civil defence centre and, after the war, a cricket training school.

Meanwhile it was decided that Eden Walk was a preferable site. The corporation already had the town's main car park there - situated on one level between 45 and 49 Eden Street - and the plan was to redevelop it as 26,000 square feet of shops and 14,000 square feet of offices, topped by a multi-storey car park. That would be phase 1. Phase 2 would entail the demolition of much of the west side of Eden Street, and its replacement with what is now Alderman Judge Mall, plus further shops and offices.

Due to a long chain of planning, property acquisitions and financial problems, work on phase 1 did not start until late 1964. It was completed in 1967, and the first occupants were John Perring, Sainsbury, Habitat, Tamplins (a long-established local chemist) the Art Shop (another time-honoured local business) and Marks and Spencer.

It was a further decade before work could begin on Phase 2. Contractors moved on site in June 1977, and a battle-weary Kingston Council announced that it would "almost certainly" never undertake such a scheme again, and all future shopping schemes would be done by private developers!

The phase 1 section was enlarged in 1983 following demolition of the old *Surrey Comet* works. The land was used for a huge Marks and Spencer extension, a new Boots store, a number of smaller shops and a realigned Pratts Passage.

In 1990 Kingston Council sold Eden Walk for £16 million to CIN Properties, part of the British Coal Pension Fund. In 2005 its long-term future was put in jeopardy by K+20, a council scheme envisaging sweeping changes to the town centre south of Clarence Street.

General Eisenhower

Tense crowds thronged Kingston Station on 6 June 1944, awaiting the arrival of the London evening newspapers. When they came the sellers were besieged, and copies were rationed to one per customer. News of D-Day was what everyone was desperate for. The previous night a huge fleet had drawn up near the French coast, with more than 700 warships escorting 2,727 ships of every kind, from sturdy Channel steamers to stately transatlantic liners, between them carrying or towing nearly 3,000 landing craft. All had sailed from the south coast of England for the Allied invasion of Normandy, and the liberation of continental Europe from Nazi occupation.

At midnight the first of 20,000 invaders' parachutes billowed into the air over France. At 6.30am the Supreme Headquarters Allied Expeditionary Force (SHAEF) broadcast to the world that "under the command of General Eisenhower Allied naval forces, supported by strong air forces, began landing Allied armies this morning on the northern coast of France."

The vast operation changed the course of World War II. News of its progress, heavily censored, held the nation in thrall, but nowhere more than in Kingston, which had secretly been involved in plotting the great exercise. The planning of the world's greatest invasion centred on a map of the region from the Normandy beaches to Luneberg Heath. And most of that map now belongs to the people of Kingston. It was dedicated to them by Eisenhower: "For the citizens of Kingston upon Thames" begins the inscription, written in Eisenhower's own hand.

49. General Dwight D. Eisenhower, future American president.

50. Telegraph Cottage, Eisenhower's retreat during the war.

Thus the General, universally known as Ike, paid tribute to the town where he lived (and secretly loved) between 1942 and 1945, and from where he masterminded much of the preparation for what was officially code-named Operation Overlord, but became known to the world as D-Day. He took command of the US forces in Britain in June 1942. Two months later he was given command of Operation Torch, the landing of Allied forces in French North Africa. His responsibilities were prodigious, and his home at the end of a gruelling day was an impersonal suite in a London hotel. The strain became so intolerable that he decided to rent a peaceful home he could call his own.

Harry Butcher, his close friend and public relations adviser, found it in Warren Road, at the top of Kingston Hill. "Ike, I've found you a dream home," he announced.

"He was right. Everything about Telegraph Cottage was right," recalled Kay Summersby, who was Ike's official driver, and the woman he came to love. She revealed their secret affair in her book *Past Forgetting*, written in 1973 when she had been given six months to live.

Kingston was unaware of its important new resident. The fact was top secret then.

"The cottage was so secret that very few people knew it existed, and even fewer knew where it was," wrote Kay." It had five tiny bedrooms and a really old-fashioned bathroom .... there was no central heating, but between the fireplace in the living room, and the big old stove in the kitchen, we were always very comfortable. There was only one telephone, a direct line to headquarters in the General's bedroom

Though Telegraph Cottage was small, it had 10 acres of lawns and woodland. Amid their peaceful seclusion, Ike was able to work out problems that had seemed insoluble in the hurly-burly of the London headquarters.

He had to leave the cottage in 1942 for operations in North Africa and Sicily. He returned to it at the end of 1943 as Supreme Commander of the Allied forces in Europe. "I'm going to move the whole shebang out to Kingston," he announced on his first day back. Thus, early in 1944, SHAEF was transferred from Grosvenor Square in London to Bushy Park, just beyond Kingston Bridge in the old borough of Twickenham.

Ike joyfully resumed residence at Telegraph Cottage. Meanwhile several of his senior staff lived nearby in Four Acres, the large house in George Road that is now Unilever's international management training centre.

Field Marshal Montgomery and other British service chiefs were frequent visitors to Telegraph Cottage, and some of the D-Day planning was done there. Years later a former gardener revealed that Ike set up a D-Day operations room in a garden shed.

D-Day came, and from then until VE Day in May 1945 Ike was mainly on the continent. But still Telegraph Cottage exerted its calming influence. On visits to Britain to confer with Winston Churchill he would snatch a few hours there, returning refreshed to France with an armful of the marrows and beans he had planted in the garden himself. Within days of victory in Europe, he flew to England and went straight to Telegraph Cottage with champagne for his private celebrations. He intended to buy the cottage, and drew up the alterations he would make there. But a new career as a statesman lay ahead, and when he left Kingston after that joyful celebration in 1945 it was, officially, for the last time.

However, he did come back, just once more. It was years later, when he had served two terms as President of the United States. He wanted to see again the house which had played such a key role in the planning of Overlord and the winning of the war.

Telegraph Cottage, whose last owner regularly opened the grounds in aid of charity, and had a plaque placed on the main frontage to commemorate Ike's tenure, was demolished in the 1980s, and the site given over to executive housing.

The Fairfield

Kingston owes this green open space to John Williams. He came to Kingston in 1851 to take over the failing Griffin Hotel in the Market Place, and made it so fashionable it attracted royal custom. He then applied his energies to town matters, becoming a councillor in 1855. Despite vicious hostility in the Guildhall from those resentful of the uneducated newcomer, without him there would have been no Fairfield today..

The Fairfield was a great open space, much larger than now, long used for grazing and agriculture. But by 1834 it was being nibbled away by building development. Williams set his heart on "enclosing the Fairfield as a recreation ground for the people," and in 1859 he formed a committee and invited subscriptions. After a promising start, the scheme was halted by public apathy and the relentless spite of his enemies.

Battered but unbowed, Williams at last got 12 acres enclosed - far less than he'd hoped for - meeting most of the cost from his own pocket. He got no gratitude. When his third term of Mayor ended, he was even denied the customary vote of thanks.

It was not until 1889 that the Fairfield Recreation Ground was properly laid out and formally opened. John Williams was not there. He had died in 1872 his end hastened, it was said, by the effort expended on his cherished Fairfield and the persecution from his foes. In his obituary, the *Surrey Comet* lamented "the disadvantages under which he laboured, and the uphill and unequal struggle he had to fight."

Freedom of the Royal Borough

The bestowing of freemanship is the highest honour in Kingston's gift, and one that is rarely given. Indeed, since the Honorary Freedom of Boroughs Act in 1885, it has been

51. The Cattle Market c.1890. The Fair was founded in 1256 and transferred to Fairfield in 1856.

conferred only 42 times in Kingston.

The word 'borough' originally denoted that its chief inhabitants were Freemen. This gave them the right to collect the 'fee farm rent' - the annual revenue due to the crown - instead of having it extracted from them by the county Sheriff, who often overcharged. King John's Charter of 1208 confirmed the right of Kingston's Freemen to govern their town without 'intermeddling' from the Sheriff. And in 1441, Henry VI granted the Freemen a charter giving them the style and title of 'the Bailiffs and Freemen of Kingston', with the right to meet at the Guildhall to make bylaws for the government of the town, and to inflict penalties on those who disobeyed them.

In Kingston Freemen also had a virtual monopoly on trade; for they were the only ones admitted to the town's four trading companies. Non-Freemen, known as 'foreigners', were forbidden to set up business unless they were granted a 'toleration'. Freemen were also excused from jury service and from paying certain dues.

After the Municipal Corporations Act of 1835, the title of Freemen went into limbo until 1885. Then, by popular request, the Honorary Freedom of Boroughs Act entitled boroughs to confer honorary freemanship as a reward for exceptional service.

Kingston's first honorary Freeman was William Court Gulley, Speaker of the House of Commons, in 1898. Others since then include the millionaire philanthropist, Andrew Carnegie; Lord Baden Powell; Earl Haig, Sir Winston Churchill and Sir Nigel Fisher.

Three of the 42 ceremonies have been confirmation of the Freedom awarded to the East Surrey Regiment in 1944, a privilege which gave it the right to march through the town with "bayonets fixed, colours flying and drums beating". This was confirmed in 1959, when the East Surreys evolved into the Queen's Royal Surrey Regiment, and again in 1993, when it became part of the Prince of Wales' Royal Regiment.

John Galsworthy

John Galsworthy (1867-1933) was born at Parkfield, a handsome house set amid rural scenery at the top of Kingston Hill. His father, John, was a London solicitor and businessman. His mother, Blanche, was a member of the genteel Bartleet family of Surbiton.

The Forsyte Saga, his most famous series of books, might never have been written had not the 2nd Duke of Cambridge begun selling off the 1,300-acre Coombe Estate he had inherited from his father in 1850. Its beauty and proximity to London, and the fact that there was a railway station close by at New Malden, made it an enticing prospect for wealthy families seeking a country seat. One of those who recognised the speculative possibilities was John Galsworthy senior, who acquired 93 acres fronting what is now George Road to build three new mansions. While the first was being built, the Galsworthys leased Parkfield (now a private nursing home, renamed Galsworthy House in the 1970s). The future author was baptised at the church of St John the Baptist, Kingston Vale, four weeks after his birth on 14 August.

The first house built by Galsworthy senior was Coombe Warren. The family moved into it before baby John reached his first birthday, and stayed until 1874. Then they moved to Coombe Leigh, the mansion John senior had built next door. Here they lived until 1878, and again from 1881 to 1886. In between they lived at Coombe Croft, Galsworthy senior's third and last Coombe development. In 1886, their children grown up, John and Blanche left Coombe to live in London.

But his happy childhood in what was then the rural beauty of Coombe, left a lasting impression on young John. This he revealed in a letter to the *Surrey Comet* in 1929. In four closely hand-written pages he spelt out

52. *John Galsworthy. Photo by Riess.*

his local connections, and those parts of Kingston which provided settings for his *Forsyte Saga.* The letter remained in the *Comet's* library files until 1979, when the paper decided to commemorate its 125th birthday by presenting it to the borough archives.

It is of particular value as the only Galsworthy manuscript material owned by Kingston. Sadly, most of his papers were bought by an American dealer. The rest are in the British and the Bodleian Libraries.

The Coombe Warren mansion, later re-named Coombe Court, was demolished in 1933. Coombe Leigh now houses Holy Cross School, while Coombe Croft is the home of Rokeby School.

Edward Gibbon

In January 1746 a small boy staggered, mute with fright, into Kingston's Queen Elizabeth's School (later re-named Kingston Grammar School). His name was Edward Gibbon (1737-94) and, according to those who knew him, he suf-

53. *Edward Gibbon, from a painting by Joshua Reynolds.*

fered "a strange, nervous affliction which alternately contracted his legs and produced excruciating pain." His schoolmates bullied him mercilessly, both for his physical handicap and his family's Jacobite leanings, while the schoolmaster, Dr Woodesson, birched him cruelly over his Latin grammar and called him "an illiterate cripple."

Nevertheless, the "illiterate cripple" went on to become one of England's great scholars, and his finest work, *The Decline and Fall of the Roman Empire,* is still unsurpassed.

Kingston had no time for him as a schoolboy, but was proud to claim him as a celebrity. His name is frequently cited in borough guides, he has a road named after him, and Kingston Grammar School's debating society is named the Gibbon Society in his honour.

Clearly he made up in brain what he lacked in beauty. The diarist, Boswell, called him "an ugly, affected, disgusting fellow" while the normally sedate *Dictionary of National Biography* states "he was ugly, and his features so overlaid with fat as to be almost grotesque.

Gibbon, who despite his unfortunate appearance was acknowledged to be "an amiable, affectionate, faithful friend, always patient, calm and industrious" would doubtless just smile to know that the school which bullied, birched and buffooned him, is now proud to claim him as one of its own!

Gladys, Countess de Grey

Gladys de Grey (d.1917), described by a contemporary as "tall and dark, a proud black swan who made any woman near her look pale", made her Kingston home a byword in 19th and early 20th century society. In 1878 she had married the 4th Earl of Lonsdale. He died in 1882, at the age of 27, leaving her with an infant daughter. Three years later she married Earl de Grey, who became 2nd Marquess of Ripon in 1909. The newly-weds settled in Coombe Court, a Kingston Hill mansion where she entertained on a lavish scale.

Noted for her beauty, wit and love affairs, Gladys also had a passion for opera, and in the late 19th century was virtually running Covent Garden. The policy of the opera house was decided by a committee of male aristocrats, whose decision on what operas were to be staged, and which singers engaged, were implemented by the theatre manager, Augustus Harris. But in reality it was the wives of the committee members who called the tune, and by far the most influential of these were Gladys and her Kingston Hill neighbour, Lady Charles Beresford.

54. Gladys, Countess de Grey at the Devonshire House ball in 1897,

In 1887 Gladys went to Brussels to hear a new singer who had recently made a sensational debut there. Her name was Nellie Melba, and Gladys was so impressed she let it be known that Augustus Harris was to engage her for performances during the current season. Harris was annoyed at being told who he should or should not hire, but had little choice but to comply. Gladys's influence was absolute.

So it was that Melba received a totally unexpected offer to sing in London. She had no idea who Gladys de Grey was, or that she had been 'secretly' discovered. Harris treated her with poor grace. His retaliation against Gladys was to give Melba's opening performance in *Lucia di Lammermoor* no publicity, with the result that the house was half empty, and the audience and the critics were lukewarm. Melba sang another two performances, then was offered the subsidiary role of Oscar in *Un Ballo in Maschera*. Her answer was to throw the first of the tantrums that later became legendary: she packed her bags and returned to Brussels.

Gladys was equally furious, and on her own initiative wrote to Melba - the first direct contact she made with her. Then came another invitation to London for the following season, couched in terms Melba could hardly refuse.

> "I know that things were badly arranged for you before," wrote Gladys. "But if you come back I promise you it will be different. You will be under my care and I shall see that you do not lack for either friends or hospitality."

It was a remarkable declaration for one of England's leading society hostesses to make to a virtually unknown singer from Australia.

Melba came back and for her opening night on 15 June, 1889, Gladys dragooned all her friends into taking seats. Dutifully they gave Melba an ovation and next morning, when the reviews appeared, she was a star.

Melba wrote years later in her memoirs: "No woman has ever had a truer friend than she who induced me to return, who stood at my side from first to last - Lady de Grey."

Not only was London's opera world at Melba's feet, but its society too. Lady de Grey virtually adopted her, and she became a permanent fixture at the parties always taking place at Coombe Court. These were legends even in their own time, and Gladys always invited the opera stars currently in town. Caruso and Melba sang duets at one of them, and on other occasions there were contributions from Chaliapin, Terazzini and the de Reszke brothers, all operatic idols of their time.

Melba later rented Coombe Cottage (which still stands in Coombe Lane West) from the Beresfords, and said the months she spent there were the happiest of her life. And when she eventually built her own house near Melbourne she named it Coombe Cottage in happy memory.

Twenty years after discovering Melba, and helping to make her the most famous diva in the world, Gladys saw Diaghliev's Imperial Russian Ballet in Paris. She was captivated, sought out Diaghilev and offered to organise a London season for him in 1911. Up to then London's experience of ballet had been solo turns in music hall bills, but now the full glory of the Imperial Russian tradition was revealed to incredulous audiences by dancers who were to become legends like Pavlova, Karsavina and, most stunning of all, Nijinsky.

So great was Gladys's enthusiasm for ballet in general, and Diaghilev and Nijinsky in particular, that she followed them all over Europe, lavishing money and holidaying with them on the Riviera. And when the company returned to London in 1912, Coombe Court became a second home for the two men, with Gladys making sure that not even the then scandalous nature of their private relationship was a barrier to their acceptance in the highest society. During that second Diaghilev season Gladys gave over Coombe Court to a grand party, organised at the personal request of Queen Alexandra so that she could meet the Russians and see Pavlova, Nijinsky and the entire company dance.

Gladys has another claim to fame: Oscar Wilde dedicated his play, *A Woman of no Importance,* to her.

Gladys died in 1917, leaving her husband to live alone at Coombe Court until his death in 1923. The mansion then passed to Gladys's only child, Lady Juliet Duff. She, like her mother, loved a social whirl and hosted parties at Coombe Court attended by King George V and Queen Mary, the future George VI, the Queen of Spain and most of the leaders of London society.

Elinor Glyn

George Road, off Kingston Hill, has many fine houses. One of them is Hampton Spring, built in 1906 for the then editor of the *Surrey Comet*, Valentine Knapp. But in 1919 the house acquired a far more exotic occupant: Elinor Glyn (1864-1943).

She had first become a household name in 1907 with the publication of her sixth novel, *Three Weeks*. That a woman should write such a full-blooded description of illicit love was unheard of, and the fact that it was an unashamed account of her own adulterous affair with a younger man outraged Edwardian society and its unwritten rule that, though one could kiss, one must never tell.

Elinor had done both, and a whole lot more, with the result that she became a social outcast with a scarlet reputation that remained with her until her death in 1943.

She had the unusual habit of receiving visitors while lying on a tiger skin rug, wearing Persian pyjamas. This inspired a

55. *Elinor Glyn, from a portrait by Philip de Laszlo.*

famous verse of the day

Would you like to sin
With Elinor Glyn
On a tiger skin
Or would you prefer
To err
With her
On some other fur?

Elinor wrote more than thirty novels with titles such as *This Passion Called Love* and *Did She?* In 1920 she left Britain for Hollywood, where she made her name as one of the first women film directors and screenplay writers. It was she who coined the now legendary term 'It' to describe sex appeal. "Of all the lovely young ladies I've met in Hollywood, Clara Bow has 'It'," declared Elinor. From then on Clara Bow became an international institution as the 'It' Girl. The word had first been used by Mrs Glyn for her book 'It', published in 1927. From that time, whether or not you had 'It' became a burning topic of the day.

In 1929 Elinor, always a spendthrift, was forced to flee the demands of American income tax officials. She returned to England, where her daughters had leased Hampton Spring for her, and decorated it lavishly in rich rose colours. She no longer received guests lying on a tiger skin rug. All the same, she must have intrigued her wealthy Kingston neighbours.

The great film star, Gloria Swanson, described her appearance: "Her British dignity was devastating. She was the first woman I'd ever seen wearing false eyelashes, and though she was old enough to be my grandmother, she got away with it. She had small, squinty eyes, and took tiny steps when she walked. Her teeth were too even and white to be real. She smelled like a cathedral full of incense, and she talked a blue streak. Her hair was the colour of red ink and she wore it wrapped around her head like an elaborate turban. She was something of another world."

The acerbic Hollywood writer, Anita Loos, was more forthright in her description: "Her appearance was bizarre. The make-up she wore might have been scraped off the white cliffs of Dover, and it provided a startling contrast to her dyed red hair, green eyes and mouth of vivid crimson. She jangled with long earrings, economically set with second-hand gems."

During her time in Kingston Elinor saw the publication of her book, *The Flirt and the Flapper*, and also directed two films at Elstree Studios. Both failed dismally and Elinor, left virtually penniless, was forced to give up palatial Hampton Spring and sell most of her possessions. Racy to the end, she died shortly before her 79th birthday.

The Guildhall

Kingston has had a Guildhall or its equivalent for more than a thousand years. A 'moot hall' is said to have been built in the 9th century, but was burned down late in the 13th century, and replaced with a 'vill hall'. This in turn gave way to a new Guildhall in about 1500. It was a picturesque, timbered building that survived for more than 300 years. But by 1838 it was so dilapidated that it was demolished and replaced by what is now the Market House, but which for 95 years was Kingston's seat of government.

Thirty years of procrastination preceded the new building and bitter argument accompanied its construction. The building committee was dissolved in acrimony, and at one point the architect, Charles Henman, threatened to abandon the scheme altogether. Civic parsimony was probably the reason. An Act passed by Parliament as early as 1808 had given the corporation authority to sell certain lands and use the cash to improve or rebuild the Guildhall. Even so, when the work eventually got under way three decades later, there was still so little cash in hand that much of the £3,800 required had to be raised by subscriptions.

The new building proved to be a bargain. It was, and still is, distinctively attractive. It was also versatile, providing market accommodation at ground level and, on its first floor, a court room and a council chamber described by a Victorian chronicler as "presenting an appearance seldom met with in chambers devoted to the meetings of municipal bodies, even in boroughs of the highest pretensions."

When the building opened in 1840, Kingston had a population of just over 8000. By 1883 that figure had increased fourfold, and a larger civic centre was demanded and discussed by councillors. However, nothing happened for the next 50 years, during which the local population soared to 106,000. At last, in January 1934, contractors began the building that was to remove Kingston's local government power base from the Market Place for the first time in its history.

Designed by Maurice Webb, and officially opened in 1935, this building is still Kingston's Guildhall. However, it was considerably extended during the early 1980s.

Douglas Haig

An estimated 45 million people observe the two-minute silence that recalls the moment on the 11th day of the 11th month, 1918, when the First World War came to an end. It is the climax of a period of remembrance of the dead of this and other wars organised each year by the

56. Kingston Guildhall, by Thomas Allom.

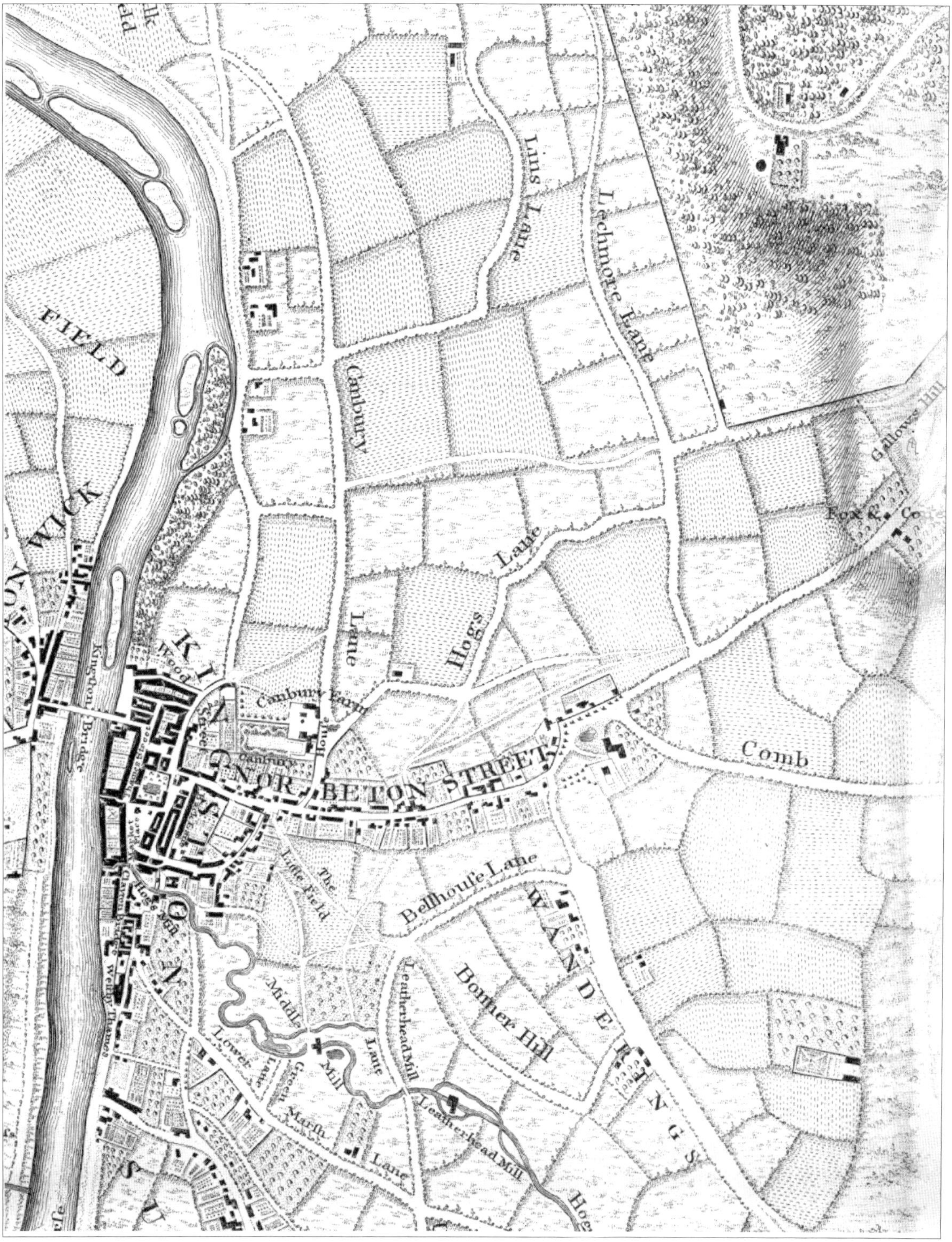

57. John Rocque's map of the Kingston area c.1745.

Royal British Legion. But the man who arguably did more than any other to win the First World War is seldom mentioned.

The Royal British Legion, which he co-founded in 1921, makes no reference to him in its information sheets, omits his name from its annual Poppy Appeal (which he launched in 1922) and has so dissociated itself from him that many staff at its HQ are unaware he was ever involved in the organisation at all.

And why does Kingston not remember him with pride as one of its most notable residents?

The forgotten man is Field Marshal Sir Douglas Haig. In 1917, when he set up home in Kingston, he was supreme commander of the British Army on the Western Front, which had two million men, and was the largest force ever fielded by Britain. The following year, against seemingly overwhelming odds, his unflinching leadership succeeded in defeating the German army.

He returned to Britain in December 1918, and met such a tumultuous welcome in Dover that, exhausted after four years' leadership at the Front, he requested a quiet welcome to Eastcott, his home on Kingston Hill.

The Mayor reluctantly dropped plans for an official reception. But workers at Sopwith's aircraft factory in Kingston, who had made a vital contribution to the war effort, were determined to honour him. That evening the entire workforce formed a procession outside the factory in Canbury Park Road. Then, led by three brass bands, and drummers and buglers from local youth groups, they set off for Eastcott to the strains of *See the Conquering Hero Comes*. Haig and his wife came out to greet them and, in an impromptu speech, Haig said this was the greatest day of his life. In response the crowd sang *For He's A Jolly Good Fellow*.

Seven months later, on 1 August, Kingston conferred on Haig the Freedom of the Royal Borough. This was the highest honour in its gift, bestowed only six times previously. The Haigs drove in an open landau to Kingston Market Place, cheered by vast crowds. Children from all the local schools were assembled along the route to sing and throw petals, and a guard of honour from the East Surrey Regiment was lined up outside the town hall, accom-

58. The scene at the reception for Earl Haig given in ??1919 at 13 Crescent Road, Kingston, home of the mayor, C H Burge.

panied by the regimental band.

Haig's Freedom document, contained in a silver casket bearing his arms and those of the Royal borough, proclaimed that "in the darkest hour he never doubted clouds would break, so under his inspiring leadership the splendid British armies in France and Flanders, who stood undaunted with their backs to the wall, doggedly confronting a menace formidable and unscrupulous beyond all precedent, and having with heroic self-sacrifice beaten off furious and repeated onslaughts, these gallant soldiers and their trusted allies sprang upon the foe, following him up and wearing him down without rest or respite, day by day, week by week, until at last Victory was achieved and Peace secured."

After the war Haig, who received an earldom in 1919, devoted himself to the welfare of ex-servicemen and their families, and founded the British Legion with Thomas Lister, an ex-army private, in 1921. He was its active president, with Lister its chairman, until his sudden death in 1928, aged 67.

His main relaxation was a game on Kingston's Coombe Wood Golf Club, where he became captain in 1922.

Until the late 20th century, the annual Poppy Appeal he launched in Britain in 1921 operated as the Earl Haig Fund, and each flower had the initials EH in its centre as proof of authenticity. Now his name has been expunged, along with the initials. The reason, say eminent military historians, is a bad press from armchair critics and damning plays such as *Oh What A Lovely War.*

According to Brigadier Brian Harding, author of the definitive history of the British Legion. "he was vilified as a heartless butcher because of his huge casualty lists. Though these accusations are grossly unfair to anyone who knows the full facts, they so discredited him that the Legion felt obliged to drop his name in case it hindered their fundraising."

Eastcott, Haig's home, was demolished for re-development several years ago. Now the only visible reminder of his presence in Kingston is his name on Coombe Wood Golf Club's wall-mounted tally of captains, and on the list of Freemen handsomely displayed in Kingston Guildhall.

Gustav Hamel

Gustav Hamel (1884-1914), one of the daring pioneers of 'flying machines', lived in The Hermitage, a large house on the corner of Portsmouth Road and Surbiton Road. A block of flats with the same name stands on the site today.

In 1911 Hamel was the first man to operate an airmail service. It ran between Hendon and Windsor, and the charge was 13 old pence per letter. In 1913 Hamel won the Aerial Derby, and in 1914 had the distinction of looping the loop 14 times in 17 minutes before King George V and Queen Mary.

Just before the outbreak of the Great War, he went to France to collect a new 80hp Morane-Saulnier monoplane. He took off in England in a thick mist and was never seen again. It seems certain that he came down in the Channel and was drowned, but this explanation was too simple at a time of such high international tension. Soon after war had been declared there were rumours that Hamel was a spy; that he was not dead, but had gone to Germany with vital military information; and that he was then flying Fokkers for the Fatherland! Another rumour declared he was the victim of sabotage. Neither theory could ever be proved.

After Hamel left The Hermitage, it was taken by the painter John McLure Hamilton (1853-1936), noted for his portraits of Gladstone, Balfour, Cardinal

59. Gustav Hamel in a Bleriot plane.

Manning, General Booth and other prominent figures of his day. Hamilton left Kingston upon Thames for Kingston Jamaica in 1933, where he died three years later aged 83.

Thomas Hansard

The announcement in 1999 that Parliament's famed Hansard reporters were being replaced by computers must have sent one occupant of Kingston Cemetery spinning in his grave. For Thomas Hansard, who edited Hansard's report of Parliamentary debates for more than half a century, spent most of his life in Kingston, and died there in 1891.

It is ironic that, though forgotten in Kingston, the name Hansard is used all over the world to denote official reports of government proceedings. Luke Hansard began printing the House of Commons Journal in 1774; but the first real reports of Commons debates did not begin until 1803, when the Press were allocated seats in the public gallery for the first time. The reports appeared in William Cobbett's *Political Register* until Cobbett was jailed for two years in 1810 for libelling the government. In 1811 he sold his business to Luke Hansard's son, Thomas, and the reports have been known as Hansard ever since.

Under the original system, newspapers were combed daily for the best accounts of MPs' speeches. These were cut out and sent to each member to revise, amend or add to what had been printed. Then the speeches were set up in type and printed in a form known as Hansard's Debates.

Thomas died in 1833, and was succeeded by his barrister son, Thomas jnr. By then Hansard was reporting proceedings independently of the daily papers, and Thomas jnr had his own reserved seat in the House of Commons. But he chose to live in Kingston because of his passion for fishing.

During his 50-plus years as editor, the Hansard publication became a national record, unrivalled for accuracy and number of volumes. Indeed, it was the only authority MPs were allowed to quote in reference to previous debates. Because it was regarded as semi-official, it was granted a government subsidy. But, to quote the *Surrey Comet* of the time, "this assistance attracted competition, and resulted in the very reluctant transfer of 85 years labour to other hands."

The 'other hands' belonged to the Hansard Publishing Union, which took over in 1889. But something went badly wrong. In its obituary to Thomas jnr, the *Kingston and Surbiton News* declared that, though he had no connection whatsoever with the Union, he was anguished by "its disastrous collapse and the disgraceful disclosures made in connection thereof" because it "dragged his long honoured family name in the mud."

His doctor was certain this hastened his end, which came at his home in Ashdown Road, on November 11, 1891. He was buried in Kingston Cemetery, and has been forgotten by the Royal borough ever since. But what was the scandal that killed him? Even the House of Commons Information Office could not give an answer!

Harding's Dyeworks

On Thursday nights a green and yellow van used to leave Acre Road, Kingston and head for the West End. It would return around midnight, laden with costumes from the Royal Opera House, the Prince of Wales, the Victoria Palace, the Garrick, the Stoll and other famous London theatres. Hours later the van would head for London again, returning the newly spruced garments to various stage doors in time for that day's performances.

This was part of the 'clean while they sleep' policy operated for years by Harding's Dyeworks, one of the most interesting firms in Kingston when the Royal borough was still enjoying its industrial heyday. It was an out-of-the-ordinary enterprise from the moment Robert Harding moved his dyeing and dry cleaning business from Hoxton to Kingston in 1859. A born showman, he became a cause célèbre through *Surrey Comet* advertisements of a sort never seen in the town before. He billed himself as 'R G Harding, the man who dyes for the ladies', and announced he had "arranged to dye daily" at his premises in Church Street. Sometimes he waxed poetic:

> "Once swains, in their ardent esteem for the ladies, would die for their smiles and descend into Hades; But I with improvement on those days that are gone; Will dye for your pleasure, yet live for my own. T G Harding wishes respectfully to remind the ladies of Kingston and neighbourhood that his dyeing struggles will be continued on any colourful pretext that they may present."

60. R G Harding & Co., dyers and cleaners in Kingston High Street, c. 1890.

In 1889 Mr Harding retired and sold the business to his son-in-law, Henry Durham. As new techniques evolved, and business increased, Harding's transferred in 1927 to premises built for them on former farmland in Acre Road. Here carpet dyeing was added to the many other specialist services, including removing the mud and grass stains from the white flannel trousers worn by Wimbledon tennis players – a highly skilled 'wet' process carried out by men wearing clogs.

During the Second World War, Harding's cleaned and dyed the uniforms of the British military as well as those of the American forces stationed in the Royal parks at Bushy and Ascot. The firm had always made a speciality of theatre contracts; and after the war Moss Bros, the famous clothes hire firm, began sending its sumptuous wedding and ball gowns to Kingston for the specialised cleaning that few other companies in Britain could offer. The firm also had a retail service, which operated under the name Trident, and had a fleet of blue and white vans calling from house to house throughout the region.

As well as costumes ranging from baggy Crazy Gang suits and animal outfits to ballerina tights and crinolines, the company cleaned, dyed and repaired the London theatres' drapery, which could be an onerous task. The Palladium's stage curtains, for example, had to be taken apart for treatment, then painstakingly stitched together again.

The firm was run by succeeding generations of the same family until it was sold in 1980. However, the new owners had taken over at a time of grim national recession and steep decline in the dry-cleaning industry as a whole. They fought back by modernising the plant and streamlining operations. But it was all in vain. In December 1981 bailiffs arrived, and a few days later the newly-formed company of Harding's of Kingston Ltd went into voluntary liquidation.

It was a sad end to a local industry that had endured for 122 years. The works was demolished in 1995 and replaced by a cul-de-sac of houses. But its name, Hardings Close, is a memorial to the unique enterprise that once stood there.

Harry Hawker

It was 12 July, 1921, a beautiful day of sunshine and light breezes, when Harry Hawker left his home in Hook Road, Surbiton and rode off on his motorcycle to Hendon airfield. He arrived at 5pm, and was soon airborne on his first test flight in a Nieuport Goshawk biplane. As England's finest pilot, he was expected to make the plane a world-beater at the forthcoming Aerial Derby.

It was not to be. At a height of about 2,500 feet, the Goshawk veered sharply to the left and dived into the ground, a large flame licking around the fuselage. Hawker, with multiple burns and fractures, died ten minutes later. He was 32.

His death was a national tragedy and King George V, and Prime Minister, David Lloyd George, were among the many to acknowledge Hawker's vital contribution to British aviation and the winning of the First World War. His loss was also deeply mourned in

Kingston. For it was Hawker's skills as an aircraft designer, engineer and pilot that helped to found one of the Royal borough's greatest industries, and he has been a local hero ever since.

But what lay behind the death of this young Australian, who had come to England in 1911 determined to master flying? The post mortem revealed that he had extensive TB of the spine and a large abcess had burst, leading, according to the pathologist, to "paralysis of the legs" and "extremely severe" pain. Thus the coroner decided that the fatal crash had been caused by Hawker's disability.

Lew Blackmore does not believe this. In his biography of Hawker, published in 1994, he says that if Hawker was in such a dire state *before* the accident, how could he have ridden his motorcycle to Hendon that day with no sign of discomfort? Also – mysteriously – the official report of the Air Ministry's Accident Investigation Branch was marked secret, and ordered to be witheld for 50 years. So it was not available to the coroner, and the real facts remained hidden until 1972. One of those facts was a defect in the plane's engine design, which did not provide for locking the carburettor tops to prevent them becoming unscrewed.

"The defect was nothing short of criminal considering there was at that time extensive knowledge of building aircraft and engines, and the need for fastening everything," writes Blackmore. The only consolation, he adds, is that Hawker would not have lived much longer in any case, given the serious disease that only became apparent during the post-mortem.

Hawker had joined Tom Sopwith's infant company at Brooklands as a mechanic in June 1912. He was taught to fly by Sopwith and in October 1912 carried out his first test flight in the new Sopwith Wright plane. In November the Sopwith company delivered its first plane to the Admiralty when Hawker flew their Tractor Biplane to Eastchurch for the handover. The price was £900, and Sopwith used the money to buy a former roller skating rink in Kingston's Canbury Park Road. Here the Sopwith Aviation Company was registered in 1913, with Hawker playing an important

61. Harry Hawker's two-hour funeral procession in 1921. Thousands gathered to pay their last respects to the heroic young pioneer of aeronautics. His coffin was borne by six staff from Hawker Engineering and a 250hp aluminium aero engined sports car laden with flowers was on the procession.

part in its development over the next seven years.

He won many competitions and set several aviation records before the First World War. In addition to flying Sopwith aircraft, his engineering skills enabled him to participate in their design. And one of his major contributions to the art of test flying was understanding the often fatal 'spin', and how to recover from it. In 1918 he was awarded the MBE for his services as a pilot.

Shortly before his death, Hawker had joined Sopwith and others in the formation of the H G Hawker Engineering Co. Its directors were drawn from the old Sopwith firm which, through no fault of its own, had been driven into voluntary liquidation at the end of World War One. Tom Sopwith took control of it after Harry Hawker's untimely death, and the name of Hawker was retained until 1977, when the company, which by then had evolved into Hawker Siddeley, was absorbed into British Aerospace.

Hawker was buried in the churchyard of St Paul's, Hook. Ennerdale, the house where he and his wife spent their brief married life, and produced two daughters, still stands close by.

High Steward and Recorder

Kingston is the only borough in the UK to appoint its own High Steward and Recorder without seeking the approval of the Crown. The earliest known reference to a High Steward of Kingston is in a document of 1579. Originally, High Stewards were appointed to preside at courts in manorial boroughs. Later the position evolved into an honorary one, held for life by people of rank and influence who could help the corporation negotiate with the government on matters affecting the town. Lord Effingham, Kingston's High Steward in 1579, being also Lord High Admiral and later Commander in Chief of forces whch defeated the Armada in 1588, was just such a man.

Until the early 20th century, most High Stewards of Kingston were peers of the realm, and were rewarded by Kingston with an annual gift of brawn, fish or wine. By 1835 this had changed to 18 sugar loaves. The current High Steward is David Jacobs CBE, DL, but no sugar has come his way. Instead he was given an illuminated scroll to mark his appointment in 2001.

The office of Recorder of Kingston is first mentioned in a charter of 1603. At that time the Recorder had to be a member of the Court of Assembly – as Kingston's governing body was known – and reside over local courts. But after the Municipal Corporations Act of 1835 the post became an honorary one. The custom of presenting the Recorder with sugar loaves upon his appointment is still observed. However he – there has yet to be a she – no longer receives a gift of brawn at Christmas.

Eminent past Recorders of Kingston include Sir Douglas Hogg and Sir Thomas Inskip, who both became Lord High Chancellor; Sir Hartley Shawcross and Sir Elwyn Jones. The last Recorder was Lord Rawlinson of Esher. He retired in 2002 and the office, customarily filled by the Attorney General, was still vacant in 2006.

The Horsefair

Since 1990 The Horsefair has existed only as a title, its original site having been obliterated by the John Lewis complex, plus the portion of the relief road that now bears its name. For centuries The Horsefair area was on the edge of the town, and used for markets and other events. Chief among these was a horse fair held in August.

62. Horse Fair shortly before demolition.

63. *Horsefair. A watercolour by W. Duncan, 1895, shortly before demolition.*

64. *River Lane in the Back Lanes, 1896.*

This later became known as Black Cherry Fair because it attracted hawkers from Buckinghamshire selling a species of small, black cherry grown in that county.

The fair came to be regarded by townspeople as an unofficial holiday, and school registers up to 1859 record the high absenteeism rate on that day. After that the fair seems to have been discontinued. School attendance also dipped on May 29, when the Ham Fair took place in The Horsefair. Travelling shows and menageries also came there, notably during the centuries-old November Fair, when Kingston Market Place and the surrounding streets were full of stalls selling toys and gingerbread.

The Horsefair was surrounded by ancient houses, shops and lanes, all of which were cleared in the 1890s, and replaced by modern buildings. It was cleared again in the 1930s, and all residents evicted without compensation or alternative accommodation, for a re-development that, because of World War Two, never materialised. The site remained empty – and used as a temporary car park – until the 1980s, when construction of the John Lewis building began. This, completed in 1990, was ingeniously designed to accommodate the section of relief road that bisects it.

The Hurricane

One of the great industrial dramas of World War Two was played out in Kingston behind the walls of the Hawker Aircraft factory in Canbury Park Road. Here men and women came from all over Britain to augment the local work force in their race to construct the Hurricane aircraft that played such a key role in the destruction of the German Luftwaffe. In shifts spread over 24 hours in a seven-day working week, the workers first raised the output of Hurricanes to 60 a month, increasing to a peak of 77 a week in 1942.

The Hurricane story began in 1933 when Sidney Camm *(qv)*, Hawker's brilliant chief designer, began development of a high performance monoplane fighter to succeed the successful Fury, launched by Hawker's in 1919. The Air Ministry was informed of the project, and officials came regularly to Kingston to inspect the timber mock-up being constructed by Camm and his team. Finally, in February 1935, the Ministry placed an order for "one high speed monoplane K5083 to design submitted 4th September 1934, known as f36/34 single seater fighter."

Construction on the aircraft had already begun, so by September it was ready for a Merlin engine to be installed. In October the prototype was loaded on to a lorry and taken to the Hawker sheds at Brooklands for final assembly and tests. It was highly advanced at that time, uniting such features as a monoplane structure, guns in the wings, a retractable undercarriage and other new features. It made its first flight on November 6 with George Bulman, Hawker's chief test pilot, at the controls. There were no spectators to see it take to the air; for, without second sight, no-one could have guessed that K5083

65. A Hawker Hurricane.

66. Poster for the Bentalls Fighting Fund, which collected enough money for a Hurricane, 1940.

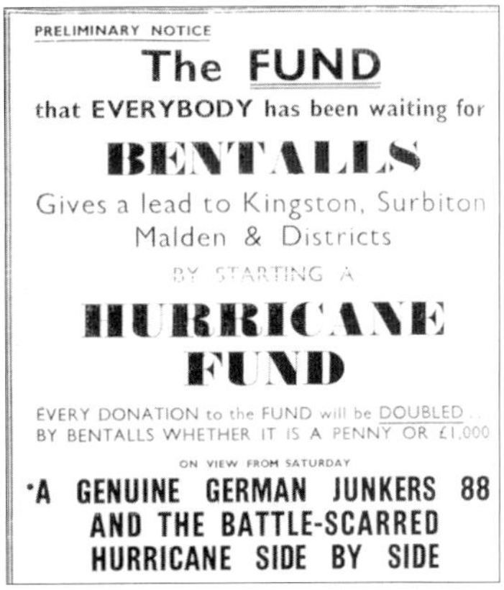

would save Britain, and change world history, as the Hurricane (the name chosen for it by Camm).

Tests proved so successful that in March 1936 Hawker's took a bold decision: with war on the horizon, and rumours of a sizeable government contract in the pipeline, they ordered work to begin on a thousand aircraft without waiting for an official production contract. It was a blessing they did. When the government ordered 600 planes in June, not only was work well in hand, but hundreds of extra craft were ready for action when Hitler launched the Battle of Britain in 1940.

When war was declared in September 1939, the RAF had received some 500 Hurricanes from the Kingston and Brooklands teams, soon followed by more from Hawker factories at Cheltenham and Slough. Indeed, it was a Hurricane from No 1 (Fighter) Squadron that claimed the first RAF kill of the war on October 30, 1939.

By the summer of 1940, the Nazis had control of Europe and Britain stood alone. It was an ideal time for Hitler to begin plotting the invasion of Britain, codenamed Operation Sealion. He set the invasion date for the end of August. But first he intended to use Germany's Luftwaffe, the finest air force in the world, to destroy the RAF, together with the UK's major ports, oilfields and defence bases. Bombs rained down on airfields from the south coast to the Tyne. They halted production of Wellington bombers at Vickers factory at Brooklands, badly damaged Croydon Airport and left a trail of death and destruction in Kingston, Surbiton and New Malden.

It was due to the Hurricane that the Battle of Britain was won. For it brought down more enemy aircraft than all the other fighter planes and anti-aircraft defences put together. Its small turning radius and devastating fire power quickly gained it ascendancy over the Germans' faster Messershmitt 10ps, while its performance at high altitude enabled it to vanquish the Dornier 17 reconnaissance machines. By mid-September it was clear that the heroic pilots of Fighter Command (immortalised by Winston Churchill as "the few") had bested the Luftwaffe. Thanks to them and the Hurricane, Hitler on September 18 deferred Operation Sealion indefinitely. Yet, perversely, it was the Spitfire that caught public imagination, and is still popularly seen as Britain's airborne saviour in 1940.

Hurricane production stopped in 1944, and the last Hurricane in RAF service retired in 1954.

Indelicate street names

Victorian delicacy caused the disappearance of some robust old street names in Kingston. The little Thames island off Portsmouth road was long known as Raven's Arse, and here were grown the osiers from which Kingston basket makers made their goods. In the 19th century, however, the name was discreetly altered to Raven's Ait – now a conference and hospitality centre. Another casualty was Kingston Bottom. The Victorians considered this obscene and changed it to Kingston Vale.

One wonders what they would have thought of "the way or lane called Shitten Lane" which is mentioned in a Canbury Court Roll of 1678. This presumably got its name from the open sewer that ran from Norbiton Street (now called Clarence Street) to Canbury Field. En route it passed through the garden of a Mr Charman, who fed his strawberry beds from it, and was widely known for the size and quality of his fruit in mid-Victorian times.

67. P. D. James.

P. D. James

P. D. James (b. 1920) began her writing career in Kingston when she was 40, and living in a Victorian cottage at 127 Richmond Park Road. At that time she was simply Phyllis White (James is her maiden name) who had struggled to bring up two daughters alone.

In 1941 she had married Connor Bantry White but, after his return from war service, he became mentally ill and was confined to psychiatric hospitals until his death in 1964. Phyllis was therefore forced to return to work in 1949 to support herself and her children. Initially she joined the health service. Then she moved to the police and criminal law departments of the Home Office.

Her first two novels, *Cover Her Face* (1962) and *A Mind to Murder* (1963), were written in Richmond Park Road. Since then all 16 of her novels have been best-sellers, she has become one of the most famous crime writers in the world, and she is one of the few authors who can claim never to have had a rejection slip.

Many writers only get true recognition after death, but she has been heaped with prizes and honours, including an OBE in 1983 and a clutch of honorary university degrees. In 1991 she was created a life peer, taking the title Baroness James of Holland Park.

Kingston Bridge

On July 17, 1828 the Duchess of Clarence left her sick bed to open the new Kingston Bridge. But the effort was too much for her, and she had return early to her home in Bushy Park. Her courage was commemorated by Kingston naming the approach road to the new bridge Clarence Street in her honour.

It had taken the town more than 600 years to achieve its fine stone bridge, and its completion was celebrated with cannon firing, flag waving and "handsome entertainments."

Kingston's original 12th-century bridge had long been both its greatest asset and biggest headache. The extraordinary thing is that the so-called 'Great Bridge', which had had such crucial influence on local and national history, was little more than a do-it-yourself affair of planks on timber stilts, ever in need of repair, and frequently closed to traffic.

This was a shocking state affairs for what was for centu-

68. Kingston Bridge, from Town End. A watercolour by M. Mackintosh, c.1850. The rutted riverside was transformed into Queen's Promenade between 1952 and 1956.

69. Kingston Bridge c.1906. Note the crowded tram on the bridge – trams were introduced in Kingston in 1906.

ries the first Thames bridge above London; and Kingston itself seems to have been to blame. Archaeologists in the 1980s unearthed 12th-century bridge remains that proved that initially only top quality materials were used. And a document of 1219 shows the bridge was well endowed with land to pay for its maintenance. That endowment was increased over the years, but suffered such mismanagement there was never enough cash to keep the bridge in order. By 1812 it was beyond repair, and there followed 12 years of wrangling, including a High Court case in which Kingston Corporation argued that the counties of Middlesex and Surrey should provide a replacement.

The Corporation lost, and in 1825 obtained an Act allowing them to build a new bridge and approach road, raising the cash by imposing tolls.

The new structure, designed by Edward Lapidge, and situated 50 yards upstream from the old one, meant razing houses, shops, inns, workshops stabling and slaughterhouses to create what was initially called New Bridge Street, but later renamed Clarence Street. Until then all through traffic had come down Clarence Street and into Wood Street before curving left into Old Bridge Street, and then over the rotting timbers of the bridge.

The total cost of the new bridge, including buying the site and approaches, was £40,000. The tolls charged to recoup some of this soon dismayed the townspeople, and one of the most joyful events in the town's annals was the day the bridge was freed from toll on 12 March, 1870.

The structure was doubled in width in 1914 and widened again 1998-2001 to provide cycle paths and five traffic lanes, including one for buses.

70. Old Bridge Street c.1895, so called because it originally led to Kingston's first bridge. John Lewis now covers the site.

71. Kingston Bypass at the Merton spur in 1934, where it was announced that a "concrete overbridge" was to be built to avoid eastbound vehicles at the spur cutting across heavy traffic to the coast. In fact it was more than three decades before it was constructed. The hoardings seen here advertise potential factory sites for sale.

Kingston Bypass

Kingston Bypass was officially born at 3pm on 28 October, 1927 when Prime Minister Stanley Baldwin stood on a patch of grass near the Burlington Road junction, cut a ribbon and declared it open. He called it "magnificent" and hoped it would be embellished with trees and shrubs and "beautiful little houses and gardens, belonging to people of all classes, coming right up to the road, carefully tended and well looked after."

He also hoped there would never be litter. "There ought to be an unwritten code that to defile roads by ugly surroundings along them, by hoggish behaviour upon them, or by upsetting and spilling litter in them should be a thing that would bar men from entering into any decent club or any decent home circle", he declared. No chance! Despite the efforts of a specially appointed 'watcher', all the trees and bulbs planted alongside the new thoroughfare by the Roads Beautifying Association were swiftly destroyed by vandals. Each time they were replaced, the wreckers struck again, usually at night.

'Hoggish behaviour' was also soon apparent. The *Surrey Comet* railed against "the flagrant violation of the law by the speed maniacs who infest our roads in ever increasing numbers", and lamented that "the new by-pass has had the effect of creating the belief among a certain type of motorist that they can indulge their craze for speed to the utmost. There have been many cases in which cars have been timed at 40 to 50mph." The Prime Minister's view that the "magnificent" road should be fringed by houses found scant support. Local opinion, led by the *Surrey Comet*, was that the road was an aberration, and that ill-judged ribbon development was largely to blame.

And so it proved. The single, 30-foot carriageway was inadequate from the start, and attempts to upgrade it have been bedevilled ever since by the buildings that soon bordered both sides. No road has attracted more opprobrium. There was no modernisation until 1958, when work began on the Hook Underpass. In the interim it was damned as a "tortuous little alley", a "wicked word", a "death trap", "skid row" and a "scar across Surrey"as it notched up an ever-mounting accident rate. But improvements could only be made by demolishing homes and annexing gardens, which inevitably

72. *Kingston Bypass 1980, no longer rural.*

sparked rage and distress.

In effect, the bypass was a casualty of the First World War, for it was originally planned in 1912 to ease increasing traffic congestion in the narrow streets of Kingston. Then came the war, and work on the road did not get under way until 1924. It was designed by the Surrey County Surveyor, W P Robinson, and was longer, costlier and more devious than the original plan. As the *Comet* remarked, "If the county council had sterilised the land required at the outset, it would have been better and cheaper than the present route. In the intervening years there had been building on an extensive scale, so many diversions were necessary."

For all its faults, the bypass was needed. In 1913 a traffic count was conducted in Kingston. By 1922 the number of vehicles had increased by 70%; by 1925 it had soared by 163%.

In the following decades the bypass was virtually submerged by traffic. Nevertheless, the first major improvement was not approved until 1954. There was then a four-year delay before work began on the Hook Road underpass and roundabout, opened by the Mnister of Transport, Ernest Marples, in 1960.

The new underpass was the first of its kind in London, with automatic lighting and heated cables beneath the asphalt to stop ice forming on the slopes. Other updates to the beleagured road gradually followed. They included the double flyover at Shannon's Corner, opened 1967, the Coombe Lane flyover (1968), and the Tolworth underpass (1970).

Kingston Crown Court

Crown Courts were born in 1972, after the Courts Act of 1971 abolished Quarter Sessions and Assize Courts, and replaced them with a single Crown Court sitting in different locations throughout England and Wales. So ended centuries of tradition in Kingston, which had long hosted Assizes and Quarter Sessions – the former attended by great pageantry, with trumpeters, javelin bearers and colourful processions.

Kingston's first Crown Court was in Canbury Park Road, in a refurbished building originally designed as a warehouse for Bentalls, and later used as an aircraft factory by Hawker's. It proved so inadequate that the courtroom at Surrey County Hall, and the Sessions House in Surbiton, had to be used as well. A new Crown Court building was opened in Penrhyn Road in 1997. It cost the Government £35 million, and was said to be the most up-to-date court house in Britain. For example, each of the 12 courtrooms was wired for playback, and four were equipped to enable child witnesses to give evidence by TV

73. *The procession of judges at the Assize in February 1968.*

link. And sophisticated technology, using cable phones and satellite, enabled witnesses to give evidence from overseas. Instead of shorthand writers there were 'cat writers', making computer assisted transcripts, and 'loggers', responsible for taping the proceedings.

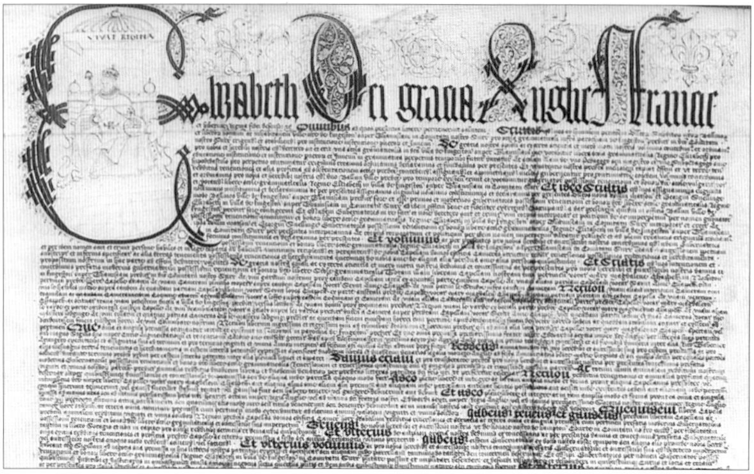

74. *The Letters Patent granted by Elizabeth I for a Free Grammar School at Kingston, 1 March 1561.*

Kingston Grammar School

In 1561 Queen Elizabeth I decreed that "there be and shall be a grammar school to endure for ever in the town of Kyngeston-upon-Thames which shall be called the free grammar school of Queen Elizabeth for the education training and instruction of boys and youths in grammar."

The school is no longer for boys only, it is not free (the fees are around £10,000 a year) and the syllabus has expanded far beyond grammar. Furthermore, the Queen's specific wish that the school be named after her has been flouted, even though there is a handsome brass plaque on its London Road frontage bearing the name Queen Elizabeth's School.

The Queen originally gave the school possession of the 14th-century Lovekyn Chapel, together with its endowments of more than 100 acres of land, 28 tenements, four inns, eight gardens and an orchard. She also stipulated that the Bailiffs of Kingston (who were elected annually, and were roughly the equivalent of today's Mayor) should be in overall charge. Thus the running of the school became vested in Kingston Council for the next 417 years.

Almost from the outset, much of the endowment was creamed off by the corporation, leaving the school with an income far lower than its founder intended. Early in the 18th century the headmaster wrote despairingly of the school's lands and tenements being "alienated and imbezzled in so shameful a manner", adding that "the money that has ever been applied to the School is nothing but the scraps and refuse of the Queen's Royal Endowment."

By 1874 the impoverished school had sunk so low that Queen Victoria assented to a scheme by the Endowed Schools Commissioners to take charge of the school and of the Tiffin Foundation, an education charity founded in Kingston by the Tiffin brothers in the 17th century. It was agreed that the endowments of the two bodies should be combined, then divided between them. At the same time many old Kingston charities were absorbed into the new scheme, and their proceeds devoted to education.

75. *Kingston Grammar School in 1795.*

This resulted in the construction of new Queen Elizabeth School buildings, opposite the original chapel premises, which opened in 1878; the creation of a new Tiffin Boys' School in 1880 and a Tiffin Girls' School in 1890. However, the bulk of the endowment funds was lavished on Tiffin at the expense of the grammar school, which eventually became so impoverished, and its pupil levels so low, it was on the point of closure. Furthermore, the fees per term at Tiffin Boys' School were £3 against the grammar school's £5, and the latter's building was described by an inspector as "quite the reverse of attractive".

76. *School pupils in 1880, and below (77), the School in London Road in 1967.*

In 1905, when pupil rolls were down to 70, the governors decided to rename the school Kingston Grammar School (KGS), launch a major fundraising appeal to upgrade the premises, and embark on other strategies to take the school into a new future.

A fundamental change to the school's original Tudor charter is that in 1978 KGS became independent, and no longer under local authority control. The move was brought about by the Labour government, which in 1975 presented direct grant grammar schools with a stark choice: go independent, or be merged into the maintained system. The KGS committee voted unanimously for independence – a brave decision that meant the loss of the Government's direct grant subsidy, and the withdrawal of free places sponsored by local education authorities. Without this large guaranteed income, a steep increase in fees was inevitable, and it was wondered whether sufficient parents of able boys would be willing to pay, given the sound education that could be had for nothing in other schools, such as Tiffin.

But there was no major independent co-educational school in the area, and KGS saw that the way forward was another fundamental change to the founding charter: to accept girls.

It proved a wise decision. Within 20 years of becoming co-ed, the school was noted nationally for its academic and sporting achievements, and by 2005 it was among the top 100 schools in Britain.

Queen Elizabeth II visited the school in 1961 for its 400th anniversary. She came again in 2005 to officially open a new £12 million extension, and to name it the Queen Elizabeth II Building. It comprises a performing arts centre with a theatre, drama department and music school, together with a sixth form social and study centre and 19 new classrooms, all built around a central courtyard.

Alumni include Edward Gibbon, and the playwrights R C Sherriff *(qqv)* and Michael Frayn.

Kingston Library

Kingston's first attempt at a free public library was made in the 1830s, when four local philanthropists established the Kingston Literary and Scientific Institute. An important feature of this was its library, open from 9am to 5pm daily, plus a further three hours in the evening. Alas, the venture was shortlived. The organisers blamed local shopkeepers who, by staying open until around 11pm each night, made it impossible for their employees to attend the institute even if they wanted to. They published

78. Kingston Library in 1903. Kingston Museum was built alongside it in 1904.

Hints to Kingston Tradesmen, exhorting them to release their employees in time to attend classes and enjoy library facilities.

"You gain gold - they lose what rubies could not buy," declared the pamphlet. "You employ them as instruments for pecuniary advantage, and so fully engross their time, and wear their bodies and minds, that they have little leisure, however great their inclination, to improve their mental powers."

So, free library facilities in Kingston disappeared for the next four decades. In 1850 the Public Libraries Act empowered corporations to levy special rates for the establishment of free public lending libraries, but Kingston did nothing about it for more than 30 years.

It was finally provoked into action in 1881, when its archrival, Richmond, opened a public library. There was much prodding of the reluctant council, led by the *Surrey Comet*, which argued in its leader column "that the amusement and instruction afforded by public libraries tend to wean youth from that idleness which inevitably leads to the commission of folly and crime."

At length the corporation agreed to act and, after much argument over a location, a library was installed on the upper floor of St James's Hall in St James's Road. It opened as Kingston Free Public Library on 6 May, 1882. The *Comet* praised it, even though "there is as yet no catalogue, no classification scheme, and only half the books are bought."

The venture, primitive though it was, was an immediate success. In his first monthly report the librarian, Mr Baxter, could boast of a total of 2,143 volumes, of which 1,382 had been bought and the rest donated. However, all donations were examined by a special committee before going on the shelves to ensure they contained nothing that might contaminate public morals. In fact, the committee was seriously concerned by the number of novels being issued by the lending department. The primary function of the library was, it felt, to provide uplifting and instructive material for the working classes to turn them from drink and vice.

By 1891 the corporation, once so reluctant, was full of pride for its library, and decided it must have better premises. The chosen building was Clattern House, an 18th-century mansion that had become semi-derelict. It stood on the site now covered by Kingston Guildhall and, even after refurbishment, fell far short of the purpose-built libraries in neighbouring areas, such as Wimbledon. However, it was all the library committee could afford from a penny rate.

79. Clarence Street from Kingston Bridge in the 1940s. The white shop building in the centre was originally the Literary and Scientific Institute. All the buildings, save Bentalls' frontage, were demolished in the 1980s.

The next major upheaval came in 1895, when the new librarian, Benjamin Carter, pressed for the introduction of the controversial open access system. We now take it for granted that when we visit a library we can do our own browsing among open shelves. In those days readers had to select books from a printed catalogue and ask for them over the counter. It was prophesied that open access would result in theft, disorder and rowdyism. Nevertheless, Mr Carter had his way so that Kingston was one of the first towns to give its ratepayers the freedom of the bookshelves. And at the annual stocktaking, only two books were missing. Kingston was also ahead of its time in encouraging children to read. In 1896 children under 14 could borrow books on the recommendation of their head teacher. But Clattern House was woefully inadequate. In 1900, for instance, it was reported that 500 children from local schools were entitled to look for books in a space only three feet square.

There *had* to be a new library. Everyone agreed on this. A site was found on the Fairfield, and architect Alfred Cox drew up plans. The big hurdle was how to raise the £8,400 needed for construction. In the event it was the stocky benefactor, Andrew Carnegie, who provided the answer – and is providing it still. For the building he funded is still Kingston's main library. It had been condemned professionally as inadequate even before it opened in 1903, yet that building, too small when Kingston had only 30,000 residents, is still the town's central library, even though the population has soared to 144,000.

Over the years there have been proposals to build a new central library on part of the former post office site in Ashdown Road. This possibility was still under discussion in 2006.

Kingston Magistrates' Court

Justices of the Peace, or magistrates, can claim a continuous history of at least 800 years, during which time they have had enormous influence on local and national life. Kingston probably had its own early form of a magistrates' court by 1199. Certainly it had one by the 1220s, and its earliest surviving court records date back to 1406. The town's long-standing right to a local justice system was confirmed by Letters Patent of James I in 1603. This made the Bailiffs, Steward and Recorder Justices of the Peace "for the Town and Liberty of Kingston, with the village and hamlets of Surbiton, Ham and Hatch, to have as full powers in this areas as the justices of Surrey in the County, including charge of the Town Gaol and power to commit felons to the County Gaol."

Typical offences dealt with by Kingston's JPs are shown in a court list for 1690:

"We present John Blake for keeping of hogs in the Kings Highway from Bishops Hall towards the Markett" and "we present George Dolley for a common swearer and cursing and damning the Court and Corporation."

Typical punishments appear in the Bailiffs' Minutes Book of the 18th century:

1705: John Turner and John Mitchell, who stole two neckcloths from a hedge, both "listed into her majestie's service", i.e. forced to join the Army.

1707: Dorothy Terrill, set in the stocks for swearing.

1710: Ann Saunders "Drunk on a Sunday by her owne Confession. Ordered to ye stocks for two houres if she can't pay 5 shillings."

The stocks, pillory and whipping post were kept in the Market Place. Public burnings were also carried out there, while hangings usually took place on a stretch of open land at the top of Kingston Hill.

Originally the courtroom formed part of the old Guildhall in the centre of Market Place. In 1811 a new courthouse opened at the south end of Market Place, but was demolished in 1933 to make way for today's Guildhall. The present magistrates' courts – threatened with closure in 2002, but later reprieved – were built alongside the Guildhall, with prison cells below, and opened in 1936.

However, in Victorian times people arrested for petty offences were often not tried in court, but taken straight to the magistrates' own homes for justice. Sir William Hardman, chairman of Kingston Magistrates, and High Recorder of the Royal borough, recalled this practice during his residence at Norbiton Hall, a mansion later replaced by an apartment block of the same name in London Road.

In 1865 he wrote: "My justice room here at Norbiton Hall has almost daily work, especially in the matter of drunk and disorderly and vagrants. I comprehend all vagrant men and women and send them for various periods to the House of Correction with hard labour. They howl and groan before me in vain, they tell piteous tales to a deaf ear. It is very unpleasant work, but is very necessary, as we are just such a distance from town as to cause us to be inundated with these wretches, and the police having got a local beak in my person, constantly on the spot, are increasing their activity."

Hardman raised hackles by becoming a JP within five months of his arrival in Kingston in 1864.

"I am told by a very good authority that my elevation to the Bench has flabbergasted several in the neighbourhood who are fully qualified and have been moving heaven and earth to get made magistrates for a long time," he wrote to a friend. "But the Lord Lieutenant would not consent, regarding their education and manners as scarcely those of gentlemen."

Today different criteria apply!

80. A covered car park was a rare amenity in 1925, so Kingston Chamber of Commerce decided to advertise the fact soon after the opening of Kingston Council's first public car park.

Kingston Market Place

The origins of Kingston Market were obscure until 1997, when archaeological excavations revealed it had been created around 1170 as the economic hub of a new town built around the existing church. For the next eight centuries it was at the core of local activity. Its merchandise, ranging from livestock and fresh produce, to fish, cloth, iron, leather, wine and cheese, brought traders and customers from far afield, and prompted the 16th-century chronicler, John Leland, to describe Kingston as "the beste markete towne in all Southery [Surrey]"

Market Place was also the seat of local government, with the town hall in its midst, and the spot where elections, proclamations, demonstrations, celebrations and most other matters of note took place.

It achieved further supremacy in 1628 when Charles II granted a charter decreeing that "no other market shall from henceforth in future be created anew, or in any manner appointed, or in any way held in any place whatsoever within the distance of 7 miles from the town of Kingston-on-Thames, either through us, or any one, of our heirs or successors."

This charter still stands, but Kingston Corporation pays it little heed. The Market Place still retains a colourful mix of stalls, but in 2003 it was controversially pedestrianised, and the stalls reduced, to provide a 'leisure space', with seats and fountains.

81. Kingston Market Place in 1800. Picture acquired for Kingston Museum in 2005.

Kingston Museum

But for a chance remark at a mayoral banquet, it is doubtful whether Kingston would ever have achieved a purpose-built museum. It was made on 11 May, 1903 by the then Mayor of Kingston, Councillor Thomas Lyne, as he hosted a nine-course feast in honour of Andrew Carnegie. Mr Carnegie had left his native Scotland some years previously, become a multi-millionaire in America, and then began devoting his riches to what he called "the vital work of bringing to the homes of the poorest and humblest people the treasures contained in books." In other words, he provided cash for towns to build free libraries.

The banquet was the culmination of a day during which Mr Carnegie had come to Kingston to open the free public library he had largely funded *(qv above)*. He was presented with a lavish address of gratitude, made an honorary Freeman and was now working his way through a gourmet menu at Nuthall's Rosebery Hall in Thames Street, while a band played mazurkas, waltzes and pizzicatos. Clearly he was delighted by proceedings.

"I was deeply impressed with the progressive character of Kingston," he wrote to the Mayor next day. "I understood you to remark that a museum was greatly needed and desired, and that ground for this had been reserved adjoining the library. I also understood you to say that if the library had been free from debt, Kingston would have erected the Museum. It would give me great pleasure as the youngest burgess to increase my gift from £2,000 to £8,000, which I understand was the total cost of the library, thus leaving you free to use the £6,000 proposed to be borrowed for your museum."

With such an offer, Kingston had no excuse for the procrastination for which it had long been noted. Architect Alfred Cox drew up plans and, on April 6 1904, a stonelaying ceremony was carried out at the half-completed building. Six months later the museum was opened by the Earl of Rosebery, High Steward of Kingston.

The *Surrey Comet* was charmed by its interior – "internally the building is in most

82. *Kingston Museum c. 1904. To the right is Kingston Library.*

respects admirable and cannot fail favourably to impress those who inspect it" - but not so sure about the exterior, commenting on the "miniature tower of somewhat incongruous design" on the roof. Nevertheless, it was considered good enough to be featured in the *Architecture Review* of 1904, and in 1992 was judged by an expert to be "a fine and slightly eccentric example of Edwardian architecture."

It is interesting to see that, whereas the benefactor Carnegie had been entertained to a nine-course banquet, the Earl of Rosebery, who did little for the Royal borough, and was described by the *Surrey Comet* as "a man who always has a past but never a future", was regaled with 11 courses!

In 1992 the museum closed for a £300,000 refurbishment - largely funded by grants obtained by its notably able administrator, Anne McCormack. It re-opened two years later with a modernised art gallery and a dynamic new permanent display telling the story of Kingston from pre-historic to Saxon times. Phase 2 of the improvements, completed in 1996, takes visitors over a bridge and into the 'Town of Kings', a display that brings Kingston's history up to the present.

Kingston has an unusually large and priceless collection of relics, artefacts, documents and pictures, some dating back thousands of years. In the Museum's earlier years, when it was run piecemeal by gentlemanly bibliophiles, most of these treasures never saw the light of day. Now, thanks not only to its visual displays, but to its local history, education, lecture, exhibition and archives services, it has enriched the social and history knowledge of students at schools, colleges, adult education classes and Kingston University, and given the public an engrossing insight into the hows, whys and wherefores of Kingston past and present. It is also noted as one of the best museums of its kind and size in the UK.

Kingston Pageant

The Pageant, designed as a re-enactment of Queen Elizabeth I's visit to the town in 1507 was held on 19 June 1917. It was, according to the *Surrey Comet,*

83. *The morale-boosting Kingston Pageant of 1917. This postcard shows the rarely depicted north side of this stretch of Clarence Street. The trees on the left mark the boundary of the parish churchyard. The road in the bottom right-hand corner is Wood Street, at this time still only a few yards wide. The Lux and Nestles advertisement hoardings are affixed to the side of the Dolphin Inn, demolished in 1936 for road widening. Beyond the Dolphin are shops which mainly survived until the 1980s, when all were demolished for the relief road and the building of a John Lewis department store.*

"as brilliant a spectacle as has ever been seen in the streets of Kingston." The Pageant was a welcome respite from the horrors of the First World War and tens of thousands of people took to the streets to see it.

Kingston Post Office

The highlight of daily life in 18th and 19th-century Kingston was the arrival of the London to Portsmouth mail coach. Drawn by four galloping horses, it would sweep into the Market Place at 10pm, the guard sounding a long brass horn, and crowds gathering to see the speedy loading of mailbags and passengers for the 70-mile journey. It was a colourful sight. Both driver and guard wore scarlet and gold livery, and the latter was equipped with pistols and a blunderbuss.

Until 1784, mail had been carried by lone, unarmed horsemen who were often robbed of their cargo. Coaches, with their trained armed guards, were not only safer and swifter, but, for the first time, gave the Royal Mail a fixed schedule with prearranged times of arrival and departure. Indeed, their reliability has never been surpassed. But their reign was comparatively brief. After 60 glorious years, they were usurped in Kingston by the railway.

Several of the town's 18th-century postmasters were innkeepers, with the post office being run from their premises, notably The Castle and The Sun, which stood within yards of each other on the west side of Market Place.

Early in the 19th century it was on the corner of Harrow Passage and Market Place (a site now occupied by Costa Coffee). Frederick Merryweather, a former editor of the *Surrey Comet*, described it in his memoirs:

> "The house was ancient in its appearance. The lower windows receded beneath the projecting upper floor; the framework was massive, and the leaden casements of the windows were filled with diminutive panels of glass."

By 1837 the Post Office had moved to Church Street. Here, on a site later acquired for major extensions to the *Surrey Comet* offices, it was run by Elizabeth Strange, who had succeeded her late father. Then romance took a hand. Thomas Baker wooed and won her, and the post office moved to his grocery shop adjoining the Druid's Head in Market Place.

Memories of this place were recounted by octogenarian George Ayliffe in a *Surrey Comet* interview in 1914: "The house was exceedingly old, with small square projecting windows and tiny panes of glass, and everything about it was old and precise. Mr Samuel Baker succeeded his father and was also a very punctual and particular man, well suited for Post Office work."

Kingston did not have a purpose-built post office until the 1870s, when one was built on the corner of Eden Street and Ashdown Road. During construction the post office operated temporarily in King John's Palace, an ancient house on the east side of High Street. The new building opened in 1876, and was designed to serve for at least 60 years. But new development, such as the introduction of postal orders in 1881, and parcel post in 1883 – after which letter carriers were renamed postmen – put paid to that idea, and in 1899 Surbiton Post Office was opened to ease the strain on Kingston. It was not enough, and in 1904 extensions were built in Ashdown Road.

The 3rd Surrey Militia barracks had previously stood here, and the former drill hall was converted into a GPO sorting office. These improvements cost £12,000, and gave Kingston one of the most up-to-date post offices in the UK. It served the town well until the Greater London Council needed part of the site for a town centre relief road. So, in 1984, the delivery depot went to a new industrial estate in Villiers Road, and in 1985 the sorting office moved to newly-mechanised premises in St Mary's Road, Surbiton.

Until then Kingston's mail had been hand sorted into pigeonholes. Indeed, Kingston was the last section of London to be converted from this centuries-old system.

The mechanised Surbiton office was the centrepiece of the SW London postal services, covering Kingston, stretching to Chertsey and Leatherhead, and handling a daily 300,000 letters delivered by 900 postmen. But its pre-eminence was shortlived. In 2001 it was merged with Twickenham sorting office and moved to the Royal Mail's new £34 million Jubilee Mail Centre, built on the site of a former rail marshalling yard at Hounslow.

Meanwhile, Kingston main

post office, reduced to counter service only, closed in 1997. Together with its ancillary buildings, it has remained empty ever since while planning schemes come and go.

However, history has, in a sense, turned full circle. In early Victorian times, Kingston's central post office was in a grocer's shop. Today it is in a corner of a self-service food store.

Kingston Register Office

Its official address is 35 Coombe Road. But to the many thousands who pass through its doors each year it is simply Kingston Register Office, where every birth, marriage and death in the Royal borough must be registered and where some 8,000 weddings have taken place during the past ten decades.

Surprisingly little is known about this building, which has no date stone, no inscribed foundation slab or any of the commemorative features usually beloved by the Victorians. Why are these offices so handsome, and of such key public importance, but sited so far from the town centre? When did they open, and who was the architect?

The answer to the first question is that it was designed as the HQ of Kingston Board of Guardians, the body responsible for Kingston Workhouse and the relief of the poor. The Board was formed in 1836, following the Poor Law Amendment Act, and was originally housed in Portsmouth Road. Over the years these premises became woefully inadequate, but nothing was done until 1897, when a site became available in Coombe Road, Norbiton. It was a perfect location, immediately adjoining the Union Workhouse, opened by the Guardians in 1839.

The original workhouse accommodated 320 paupers, and was so handsome that disgruntled ratepayers dubbed it 'The Grand Palace'. Other buildings were added over the years, all designed to harmonise. Thus, when the Guardians finally embarked on their much-needed new base next door, it had to be of matching quality. Architect William Hope made sure it was. Described as 'late gothic', it was constructed of red Bracknell bricks and Bath stone, and is still Norbiton's most stylish landmark.

Twenty firms competed for the work, from which Messrs John Shelbourne of Southend were chosen. Three months later they lost the contract to Meredew and Worth, who soon went bankrupt. Eventually, the greater part was built by W Brooking of Richmond, who had trouble obtaining the special stone for the imposing main entrance. The new quarters were completed by October 1900 at a cost of £7,450 (excluding the site) and 60 candidates applied for the post of caretaker. With the position went a two-bedroom flat on the second floor, which remained the caretaker's residence until the job was abolished in 1998.

And the link between the Guardians and marriage? That goes back to the Civil Registration Act of 1836, which for the first time allowed weddings to take place in 'register offices' as well as places of worship.

In Kingston the Guardians seem right from the start to have shared their premises in Portsmouth Road with the Superintendent Registrar of Marriages – perhaps because both the Poor Law Amendment and the Civil Registrations Acts were passed in the same year.

It is interesting to note that in the 19th century only one marriage in a hundred was a civil ceremony, and Kingston's first Register Office wedding did not take place until 17 July, 1845.

Meanwhile the Registrar for births and deaths was based a mile away in Cromwell Road, where he remained until transferred to the Coombe Road building in 1916.

Legislation in the 1990s meant couples could wed in any register office without residential qualification. It also enabled hotels, stately homes and many other places besides churches and register offices to be licensed for weddings. The result is hot competition between marriage venues, and Kingston Register offices, previously the scene of up to 800 marriages a year, has seen a big drop.

However, it is still one of the more imposing register offices in the UK. The original building, with its fine internal pilasters, columns, arches and beautiful windows, has been preserved intact, even down to the marble fireplaces and brass door furniture.

84. Kingston Railway Station c. 1904.

Kingston Station

There is a popular myth that the corporation was so opposed to the London & Southampton Railway running its line through the town with a railway station there, that the company rerouted it to Surbiton instead. However, this is an exaggeration, for the Company's original route did not pass through the town centre and did not include a central station. After Wimbledon, it would have crossed Coombe Lane and Norbiton Common, and continued north of the junction between what are now the Dickerage and Kingston Roads. Then it would have crossed the Hogsmill and skirted Surbiton Hill. The station that Kingston refused would have been close to the Waggon & Horses at the foot of Surbiton Hill, about a mile from the spot where the station of New Kingston opened in 1838. Initial post-railway development would therefore still have been centred on Surbiton, and the dire effect on Kingston's trade and industry would have been the same.

The first Kingston/Surbiton Station was placed deep in a cutting to the west of the present Ewell Road Bridge, but was little more than a hut. The Vauxhall to Woking portion of the line opened in 1838 to coincide with Epsom Races. *The Times* of 31 May reported: "... At an early hour upwards of 5,000 persons assembled at the gates of the Southampton Railway near Vauxhall for the purpose of going by the railroad trains to Kingston Station, and from thence by other conveyances to the race course. There were ten times more applicants for seats in the train vans than there were seats for their accommodation. The proprietors did what they could to meet the demands for conveyance, but they could not do what was impossible."

The Company's first timetable had five trains daily each way on the new line, and thirty-one minutes were allowed for the ten miles between Nine Elms and Surbiton at a fare of 3s first-class and 1s 6d for second.

Journalist Frederick Merryweather recalled that the guard sat on the roof of the train, working a primitive brake. "Night or day, through wind or storm, through tunnels and the bleakest country, smothered with smoke or blistered with sparks and dust, the poor guard was often so perished and benumbed as to be unable, when he reached the terminus, to leave his seat without help."

In 1839 the London & Southampton was renamed the London & South Western Railway and the following year the 77-mile line from London to

LONDON & SOUTHAMPTON RAILWAY.

The London and Southampton Railway IS NOW OPEN for the conveyance of Passengers and Parcels from London to Woking Common (near Guildford), and the intermediate places.

The times at which the Trains will start are as follow:

FROM LONDON.		FROM WOKING COMMON.	
Morning	8	Morning	half-past 7
Ditto	10	Ditto	10
Afternoon	1	Afternoon	1
Ditto	half-past 3	Ditto	half-past 3
Ditto	6	Ditto	7

EXCEPT ON SUNDAYS,

When the Trains will start

FROM LONDON.		FROM WOKING COMMON.	
Morning	7	Morning	7
Ditto	9	Ditto	9
Afternoon	5	Afternoon	5
Ditto	7	Ditto	7

The Fares will be charged as under, viz.

From the Terminus at Nine Elms,
NEAR VAUXHALL,

	FIRST CLASS £	s.	d.		SECOND CLASS £	s.	d.
To WOKING COMMON	0	5	0	-	0	3	6
To WEYBRIDGE	0	4	0	-	0	2	6
To WALTON	0	3	6	-	0	2	3
To DITTON MARSH	0	3	0	-	0	2	0
To KINGSTON	0	2	6	-	0	1	6
To WIMBLEDON	0	1	6	-	0	1	0
To WANDSWORTH	0	1	6	-	0	1	0

No Fee or Gratuity will be allowed to be received by any Servant of the Company.

Times at which the Trains are appointed to arrive at the undermentioned Stations, until further notice:

DOWN.

FROM Nine Elms / ARRIVE AT	Miles.	8 A.M. h. m.	10 A.M. h. m.	1 P.M. h. m.	3½ P.M. h. m.	6 P.M. h. m.
Wandsworth	2¾	8 7	10 7	1 7	3 37	6 7
Wimbledon	5¾	8 18	10 18	1 18	3 48	6 18
Kingston	10½	8 31	10 31	1 31	4 1	6 31
Ditton Marsh	12¾	8 41	10 41	1 41	4 11	6 41
Walton	15¼	8 51	10 51	1 51	4 21	6 51
Weybridge	17¼	8 59	10 59	1 59	4 29	6 59
Woking Comm^n.	22¾	9 15	11 15	2 15	4 45	7 15

UP.

FROM Woking Comm^n. / ARRIVE AT	Miles.	7½ A.M. h. m.	10 A.M. h. m.	1 P.M. h. m.	3½ P.M. h. m.	7 P.M. h. m.
Weybridge	5½	7 44	10 14	1 14	3 44	7 14
Walton	7½	7 51	10 21	1 21	3 51	7 21
Ditton Marsh	10	8 1	10 31	1 31	4 1	7 31
Kingston	12¼	8 10	10 40	1 40	4 10	7 40
Wimbledon	17¾	8 26	10 56	1 56	4 26	7 56
Wandsworth	20	8 35	11 5	2 5	4 35	8 5
Nine Elms	22¾	8 45	11 15	2 15	4 45	8 15

85. *Fares and timetable for the Vauxhall to Woking railway, 1838.*

86. *Kingston station commuters in 1934. Note the virtual absence of women.*

87. *Kingston Station today. It was rebuilt in 1934.*

Southampton completed. In 1848 the London terminus was moved from Nine Elms to Waterloo. Meanwhile, Surbiton's crude little station, reached by a steep descent down the embankment from South Terrace, was replaced.

Trade, property values and life generally in Kingston proper were affected by the station at Surbiton. Even so, thousands signed a petition of protest when the LSWR announced it would form a short branch line, starting at Twickenham, and coming over the river to central Kingston via Hampton Wick. Indeed, the *Surrey Comet* remarked on "the opposition the company have uniformly met with at the hands of the majority of townsfolk." Nevertheless, on 19 May 1861 work began on the rail embankment on the Kingston side of the river in what is now Skerne Road. The line was carried on an arch over the road and the new Kingston Station was built on the site of what had been one of the largest tithe barns in the country.

This new line opened in 1863, with fifteen up and thirteen down trains to and from Waterloo via Richmond. An electrified service was inaugurated in 1916 with a train every ten minutes, with the first each day leaving at 4.21am.

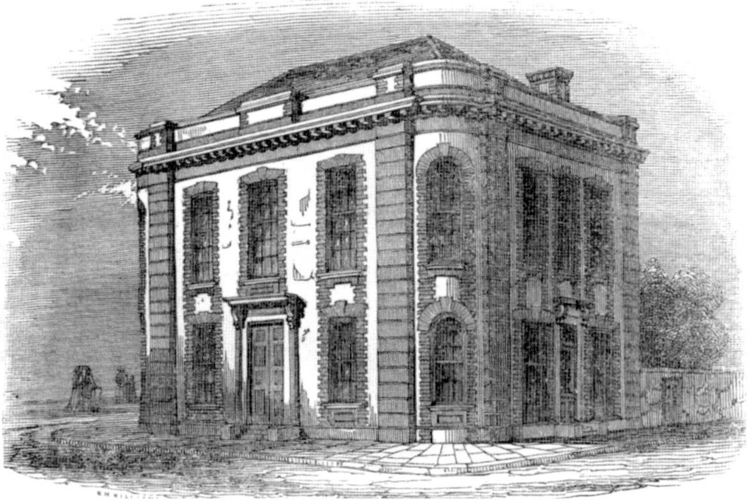

88. *The Kingston Literary and Scientific Institute.*

89. *Kingston Science, Art & Technical Institute, forerunner of Kingston University and Kingston College, in Kingston Hall Road.*

Kingston University

The roots of Kingston University stretch back to 1839, when four leading townsmen established the Kingston Literary and Scientific Institute to provide evening classes for young men. It was a hand-to-mouth affair at first, with meetings held in any room that happened to be free. Then Dr George Taylor, a surgeon who lived in a house adjoining Kingston Bridge, paid for purpose-built premises for the Institute. These opened in 1841 at the corner of Thames Street and Clarence Street, and consisted of a handsome neo-classical building containing a library, laboratory and lecture hall.

The Institute lasted only eight years – partly because so many youths were kept at work by their employers until 10pm each night and partly, in the words of a contemporary, "owing to the disinclination of the young men of Kingston to take part in anything which had a semblance of education or mental improvement about it." Thereafter the Institute building served as a shop until its eventual demolition in the 1980s.

But the venture was not the failure it seemed at the time. It had planted a desire for further education in people's minds and a few years later the Mechanics' Institute was launched in rooms over a shop in Church Street. Then in 1870, following the Elementary Education Act, evening classes in science and art were established at the national schools in Wood Street, and a Polytechnic Institute was opened in Fife Road.

These early efforts paved the way for Victorian Kingston's ultimate in further education: the Science, Art and Technical Institute, which opened in Kingston Hall Road in 1899 on a site now occupied by Kingston College.

In 1930, after student rolls had vastly increased, it was split into two independent units, the School of Art and the Technical College. In the mid-1960s the Technical College was divided into Kingston College of Technology and Kingston College of Further Education. This family tree took another turn in 1970, when the College of Technology and College of Art reunited to form Kingston Polytechnic. Five years later they were joined by Gipsy Hill College of Education, which had been established in South London in 1917, and transferred to Kingston in 1946.

The Polytechnic flourished in a way that would have thrilled Kingston's further education pioneers of 1839. In the two years before it became a university in 1992, it was rated as England's top polytechnic. And in 1994, when Sir Frank Lampl was installed as the first chancellor, it was acknowledged to be among the top five of Britain's 41 new universities.

By the start of 2005, Kingston University had nearly 18,000 students, with sites at Penrhyn Road, Kingston Hill, Knights Park and Roehampton Vale. Plans were also well in hand for it to buy the former

Surrey County Hall, a listed landmark building in Penrhyn Road intended, after complex interior alterations, to be its principal base. The purchase would be largely funded by selling the Knights Park campus to developers. These plans came to an abrupt halt in January 2006 when Surrey County Council decided not to vacate the building after all.

Meanwhile Kingston College of Further Education became Kingston College in 1993. It still occupies the original 1899 site in Kingston Hall Road, but the old premises were demolished in 1972 and replaced by new ones, including an 11-storey tower block, whose outward appearance (it has been dubbed the ugliest blot on Kingston's townscape) belies the well planned interiors. There have been further additions in the 21st century, including a large sports hall opened in 2003 and a theatre and engineering workshops completed in 2005. It currently (2006) has 8,371 students, and offers courses up to degree and post-graduate level.

90. A view of Kingston in the 1890s looking north from the parish church tower. In the immediate foreground beyond the churchyard trees is Clarence Street and a line of buildings that stood until the 1980s. Immediately behind is the ancient Horsefair area, which was soon to be swept away. Just beyond the Horsefair, in the centre, is

Listed Buildings

For most of the 20th century Kingston was so heedless of its heritage that it had fewer listed buildings than any other London borough. The town was well on the way to being laid waste environmentally and historically when, thanks largely to pressure groups like the Kingston Society, a conservation division was established at the Guildhall in the 1980s.

Successive conservation officers have done their job so well that by 2005 the Royal borough could boast 180 listed properties compared with only 11 in 1970. It also had nearly 200 'Buildings of Townscape Merit' and 26 conservation areas (there were none in 1970) containing 6,154 properties.

Grade I listings are buildings of outstanding interest, deemed of paramount importance to the nation. Central Kingston has two of these – All Saints Church and Clattern Bridge. It also has two Grade II starred buildings: Cleave's Almshouses and the Lovekyn Chapel, both in London Road.

Grade II listed buildings in the town centre include Siddeley House, an office building in Canbury Park Road that was formerly Sopwith Aviation's experimental workshops; 23 Market Place, originally an ancient inn called the Queen's Head but now a fashion shop; The Wood Street frontage of the Bentall Centre, designed by Maurice Webb in the style of the 17th-century portion of Hampton Court Pal-

Nightingale's Brewery, which was also about to disappear. Immediately beyond that is Marsh's corn mill. On the far right is a glimpse of Wood Street, then only a few feet wide, still containing a handsome vicarage set in tree-studded gardens. Later, all that side of Wood Street would be covered by Bentalls. Nothing in this picture survived the 20th century except the railway bridge over the Thames.

ace and the former Granada Cinema, now Oceana night club, in Clarence Street.

2nd Earl of Liverpool

A long procession set out from Kingston Hill on 15 December, 1828. The 2nd Earl of Liverpool (b. 1770), the second longest-serving Prime Minister the country had ever known, had died at his residence, Coombe House.

The elaborate arrangements for his funeral were entrusted to Henry Knight, who had a drapery and undertaking business in Kingston Market Place. Friends and relations had decreed that no expense should be spared in honouring the memory of a man who had served 15 years as Prime Minister, and was one of the ablest speakers of his day. Some idea of the procession is given by these three expenses: "Sundry bills at inns on the journey for all the attendants, horses etc, £246.12s. Keep of the 12 saddle horses on the journey, ostlers etc £24. Refreshment for the pages, porters and servants while at Kingston the morning of removal from Coombe Wood, £18s. 10s."

The Earl was interred in the family vault at Hawkesbury, but in Kingston he is remembered in the name of Liverpool Road, which stands on what was once part of his farm in Kingston.

91. Robert Banks Jenkinson, Earl of Liverpool.

Lord Liverpool, who became Prime Minister when only 42, married twice. His first wife was Louisa Theodosia, daughter of the 4th Earl of Bristol. A life-size statue of her by Sir Francis Chantrey stood for years in the entrance hall of Coombe House. Ultimately it was given to Kingston parish church, where the Earl was a worshipper. It remains there still as one of the building's finest memorials, with an inscription that reflects her virtuous life: "She visited the fatherless and widows in their affliction, and kept herself unspotted from the world."

Lord Liverpool's chief hobby was farming, and in Kingston he owned Park Farm, which extended from today's Kings Road to the boundary of Richmond Park. He was High Steward of Kingston from 1816 until his death, and was known for his generosity to the poor people of the town.

Coombe House, where he entertained many kings, princes and emperors, was demolished in 1933, but its lodge and much of its boundary walling remain.

Margaret Lockwood

Margaret Lockwood (1916-90), who lived the last 30 years of her life in Kingston, was the most popular British film star of the 1940s, and at the height of her career acquired legendary status with such films as *The Man in Grey* (1943) and Alfred Hitchcock's *The Lady Vanishes* (1938). But it was her starring role, together with James Mason, in *The Wicked Lady* (1945) which established her, uniquely among British actresses of the time, as not only glamorous, but dangerous and sexually seductive as well.

She was the first British actress to be groomed specifically for screen stardom, and made her film debut in *Lorna Doone* in 1934, when she was 19. She appeared in 44 further films, her last being *The Slipper and the Rose* in 1976.

She moved to Kingston in 1961, and home for the rest of her life was a 1920s house in Upper Park Road, a cul-de-sac abutting Richmond Park. During her career she appeared in 26 stage plays, eleven of them while living in Kingston. Her final stage role was in *Motherdear* at London's Ambas-

92. Margaret Lockwood, famous for her beauty spot.

sadors Theatre in 1980 in which she played Queen Alexandra. After that she became semi-reclusive, and refused all film, stage and television offers.

Looker's Pottery

One of the features of Kingston Hill is a lake, set amid lawns half-way up the hill. It now forms part of the gardens of Lakeside, a development of high-rise flats. But it was not, as often supposed, the creation of a landscape gardener. It is, in fact, the only reminder that this land was once part of Looker's Brickfields and Pottery, a famous concern that supplied many parts of Britain with bricks, tiles, flowerpots and earthenware artefacts of many kinds.

The firm was founded in the 1830s by Benjamin Looker. He was a builder by trade and his home in Clarence Street had a yard and works at the rear. Queen Victoria had not yet been crowned when he acquired several acres on what were then the wild and lonely slopes of Kingston Hill. It was heavy clay land, and here Mr Looker established brickfields on a site extending from what is now the Albert Hotel up to what is now Crescent Road. He sold his Clarence Street business, and settled at Claylands, an aptly-named house which stood opposite the brickfields, close to where Wolverton Avenue is today.

Looker soon became a household name, largely because of a special type of hollow earthenware garden tablet which he invented and patented. This, inscribed with any wording the customer chose, became popular, and many thousands were despatched each year from the kilns on Kingston Hill.

In later years Mr Looker became tenant of Park Farm, formerly owned by Lord Liverpool. This lay mainly on the north side of Kings Road, and was richly fertile. But when the Kingston railway line was extended to join the main line at New Malden in the late 1860s, the farm's cornfields were eagerly snapped up as building land.

Much of the site was acquired by the British Land Company, which by the spring of 1869 had begun covering the fields with a network of residential roads. Kingston Barracks was built on the site of the old farmhouse in 1875.

When Mr Looker retired, the business passed to his eldest son, Benjamin, and his younger twins, William and James. Benjamin junior used many of the famous Looker bricks to build himself a home on the edge of the brickfield. He called it Cromwell House, and today its site is occupied by the apartment block, Cromwell Court.

Eventually the Looker land on Kingston Hill was 'worked out' as far as brickmaking was concerned, and Benjamin and his brothers established fresh brickfields on Norbiton Common, the windswept tract of farm and open land which at that time separated Kingston and New Malden. The climax of Benjamin's career came in 1884, when he secured 14 acres of meadow which had formed part of Blagdon Farm, New Malden. This had been occupied for many years by a Farmer Raynes, after whom the Raynes Park district is named.

Looker's Blagdon Road brickfield flourished until Benjamin's death in 1892. Then it was sold, becoming the New Malden Potteries and, later, Norbiton Potteries.

Meanwhile, Looker and bricks were still synonymous. The twins, William and James, were still operating on Norbiton Common under the name Looker Bros, and there they stayed until their retirement in 1906. Now the land they worked so long is covered by a dense network of residential roads, and no-one would guess that such an area as Norbiton Common ever existed. But there is one memorial to the Looker enterprise: the name of Potters Grove.

Meanwhile, the Blagdon Road pottery continued for several more years. By the 1920s the clay pit was exhausted. Then came news that the London Underground was being extended from Clapham to Morden, and massive quantities of unwanted clay were being excavated. The pottery asked to have it, and soon the pit had been refilled, and the company paid a handsome fee for taking the clay.

By 1938 the clay was again almost exhausted, and the pottery was confined to making flower and chimney pots. However, with the outbreak of World War Two, the brick-drying machines sprang into life once more when the firm secured a contract from the Ministry of Food to dry out cereals damaged by sea water, or during air raids.

Finally, 60 years after Benjamin Looker had founded it, the brickworks came to a

93. *Lovekyn Chapel, by James S. Ogilvy, published in 1914.*

dramatic end, symbolised by the demolition of its giant chimney stack in 1945. The event made national news, and children were given time off school to witness the event.

Now the old brickfield is the site of some of New Malden's most modern buildings, including a multi-storey car park that would have made a fortune for Benjamin Looker had he been able to supply the bricks!

Lovekyn Chapel

It was an unromantic wedding. The 60-year-old bridegroom had fathered 13 children and was still in love with the memory of his first wife. His 16-year-old bride was a substitute for the beauty he had really wanted to marry. Yet the marriage of Edward I and Margaret of France proved surprisingly happy, and also led to the building of a unique historic monument in Kingston.

The wedding took place in Canterbury in 1299, followed by a feast provided by a Kingston caterer named Edward Lovekyn. He produced a lavish spread, but the King was slow to settle the bill - about £50,000 in today's values. Eight years later the King died, and the debt passed to his son, Edward II.

Lovekyn offered to cancel the debt if the new monarch would allow him to found a chapel in Kingston. Edward II agreed, and the result was the Lovekyn Chapel, now thought to be one of only two surviving free-standing chantry chapels in England. A chantry chapel could only be built with Crown permission, and its sole purpose was to be a consecrated spot where appointed priests prayed for the souls of its

94. The Lovekyn Chapel, original home of Kingston Grammar School, later became the school's carpentry workshop until 1992.

founder and his family. Most were attached to a major church, and it was rare for anyone to be allowed to build a separate one.

The Lovekyn Chapel's religious life ended in 1547 when Edward VI abolished chantries. It began a new career in 1561, when Queen Elizabeth I decreed that the chapel and its endowments be given over to "a grammar school ... which shall be called the free grammar school of Queen Elizabeth for the education, training and instruction of boys and youths in grammar."

Thus began what is known today as Kingston Grammar School *(qv)*, which has owned the Chapel ever since. Early in the 1990s the building was restored and refurbished and is now available for hire as a small concert or lecture hall.

95. George Meredith.

George Meredith

Kingston lost a distinctive landmark in 2005 with the demolition of Kingston Lodge, which was built for - and probably designed by - Charles Molloy Westmacott in 1838. He came from a family of distinguished sculptors, artists and architects, and Kingston Lodge when he lived there was a picturesque country residence with large gardens, an ivy-clad tower embellished with battlements, and an entrance lodge at what is now the junction of the London and Coombe Roads.

It captivated novelist and poet George Meredith (1828-1909), one of the major literary figures of the age. In 1864 he married for the second time (his first wife had eloped with an artist six years previously) and the newly-weds decided to settle in Kingston. First they took lodgings. Then, finding Kingston Lodge vacant, they took it on a three-year lease as their first settled home. Meredith declared that "comfort, fortification and gentlemanliness made the place an ideal English home."

Before and after. 96 above is Meredith's house at 142, London Road (Norbiton/Kingston?? Lodge). Below (97) is the ruin it became. A block of flats called Buick House, was completed on its site in 2006.

Here they entertained many of the most famous literary and artistic figures of the 19th century, here their son William Maxse was born in 1865 and here Meredith completed his novel, *Rhoda Fleming*, wrote most of *Vittoria* and a large portion of *The Adventures of Harry Richmond*.

The Kingston Lodge idyll was short-lived. "I like nothing about Kingston he wrote in 1865. "But I have determined to save up, and put by, and endure this place (if possible) for the three-year term, and when I move it will be to a fixed place."

The main reason for Meredith's hatred of Kingston was St Peter's church, a few yards from his home. The noise of the organ, and the hell-fire-and-damnation roarings of the vicar, a dedicated evangelist, were so intrusive that they finally drove the Merediths out before their lease expired.

They settled in Box Hill, near Dorking, where Meredith died 40 years later.

In its last years Kingston Lodge was a mutilated remnant of its original self. It became home to an engineering business, and the drawing room, where Meredith entertained the pre-Raphaelites and other great names, was a motor repair shop, with fragments of the elegantly moulded ceiling still surviving above the work benches. The front garden was replaced by vehicle showrooms, and the back one by a supermarket unloading bay. By the close of 2005, a large apartment block, Buick House, was nearing completion on the site.

The Military

Kingston has a military history stretching back to Saxon times and countless townspeople down the centuries have stood up to whoever was threatening Britain at the time. The genealogy of the Princess of Wales's Royal Regiment is too complex to detail here. Suffice to say that, through centuries of regimental marriages and births, it is still linked to the 'fyrd' – the militia established to repel invaders in the Saxon era, long before there was a regular army.

There have always been soldiers in Kingston because of its strategic importance. Regular troops were stationed in the

Camberwell). This meant extending the town's military HQ so the premises could "provide a place for keeping arms, accoutrements, clothing and stores", plus rooms for orderlies and guards, a magazine and "a sufficient yard or place for men to be mustered for issue and return of arms."

Army reforms in the 1870s made accommodation for the armed forces a government, rather than a county, responsibility. They also 'territorialised' the regular army by giving regiments a geographical link with the counties whose names they bore, and created a link between the regular and volunteer forces. As part of this policy the War Department bought 16 acres of farmland for the building of Kingston Barracks in Kings Road.

The new premises were designed by Major Siddon of the Royal Engineers, cost £40,000 and, when completed in 1875 were described by the *Surrey Comet* as "the last word in barracks building." Initially it was a brigade depot centre, where recruits for the 70th (Surrey) Regiment, then serving in India, and the 31st (Huntingdonshire) Regiment, then in Gibraltar, trained. These old numerical titles were abolished in 1881, and the 32nd and 70th merged to form the 1st and 2nd battalions of the new East Surrey Regiment, with Kingston Barracks as its depot.

The East Surreys, known affectionately as Kingston's Own Regiment, made a huge military contribution to the two world wars. For example, in the World War I, more than 84,000 men marched to battle through the barracks' massive keep

98 and 99, two scenes from Kingston Barracks on 1 May 1959, on the occasion of the last passing-out parade of the East Surrey regiment. The regiment was then amalgamated with the Queen's to form a new regiment based in Canterbury. The salute was taken by Brigadier G. Roupell, colonel of the East Surreys, and the parade commander was Captain K. Osborn.

town in 1685, and in 1782 a depot company for the 70th (Surrey) Regiment was established here.

In those days regular soldiers were billeted in pubs and private houses (the landlords and householders having no say in the matter) while the militia and volunteer units, being local, usually lived at home. So barracks, as such, were not required until Victorian times. Kingston's first barracks opened in 1855 in what had been the old county jail in Eden Street. It housed the county militia, and Surrey paid £2,300 for the jail and £1,960 for its conversion.

In 1859, Napoleon III's warmongering in Europe led to such unease that a corps was enrolled at Kingston in 1860 as the third of the four battalions of the East Surrey Brigade (the others were based at Wimbledon, Clapham Common and

100. National Service Recruits march to Kingston Station from the East Surrey's Regimental depot in Kingston. The picture was taken in Richmond Road in 1956.

gates. Nearly 7,000 were killed, and many more horribly injured. And thousands more served in World War II.

Many acts of heroism went unrecognised in the bloody chaos of the First World War trenches. Even so the East Surreys achieved a remarkable tally of 62 battle honours, including seven Victoria Crosses – the highest military award for gallantry.

In 1944 Kingston Council decided to show its appreciation by presenting the regiment with the Freedom of the Royal borough – an honour it had never before conferred on any military or other corps. This gave the regiment the right to march through the borough with "bayonets fixed, colours flying and drums beating", but because of the war the formal ceremony had to be postponed until 1947. There was an even more splendid day in 1952, when the regiment exercised its marching rights before Beating Retreat on the barracks' parade ground with the massed bands of the regiment and the Royal Marines.

The East Surrey's last major public appearance in Kingston was its Freedom March on June 20, 1959. Four months later it was merged with the Queen's Royal Regiment to form the Queen's Royal Surreys, and Kingston Barracks were closed. In 1992 the regiment became the Princess of Wales's Royal Regiment, and Kingston Council re-conferred the Freedom on them in 1993.

Kingston Barracks were demolished, and replaced by army married quarters in the 1970s. But the handsome keep has been retained as a historic landmark.

William Millais

His name is little known. But William Millais (1828-99) was as talented an artist as his world-famous brother, John Everett Millais, co-founder of the Pre-Raphaelite Brotherhood. Indeed, it is said he would have become the greater of the two had he chosen to concentrate on painting. Instead he preferred to use his outstanding musical talents locally, organising high quality concerts in Kingston and singing in the choir of St Mark's Church, Surbiton.

Sir William Hardman, a leading local and national figure, wrote in 1855: "...we have

101. This watercolour by William Millais, depicting the river scene from near his home in Portsmouth Road, was bought by Kingston Museum in 2003 with public donations and a grant from the V & A Museum.

some rare singers here in Kingston, among whom the chief is William Millais, the brother of the celebrated J E Millais, and perhaps the finest amateur tenor in the kingdom."

On another occasion Hardman wrote to a friend: "William Millais called on us the other day....He is full of fun and conversation and has one of the most beautiful tenor voices I ever heard."

William spent some time with the Pre-Raphaelite Brotherhood at Worcester Park Farm, where he produced watercolour landscapes. He also exhibited at the Royal Academy between 1852 and 1892. But music and the cultural life of Kingston were his first loves.

Fortunately Kingston Museum was able to acquire one of his watercolours *(ill. 101)* in 2003. It was painted in the 1850s from a spot close to the family home in Portsmouth Road, and is a view of the Thames with Kingston Bridge visible in the distance.

Monday Market

In 1925 Kingston's weekly cattle market was transferred from Kingston Market Place to Fairfield North, where it continued as a major local event for the next few years. However, it was abandoned after the Second World War, when most of the farmland that had once bordered the Royal borough had been swallowed by roads and housing. But the site is still called the Cattle Market, and a general market is still held there each week. Known as The Monday Market, it boasts more than a hundred traders and draws thousands of shoppers from all over the South East.

102. The Monday Cattle Market at Fairfield West in 1945.

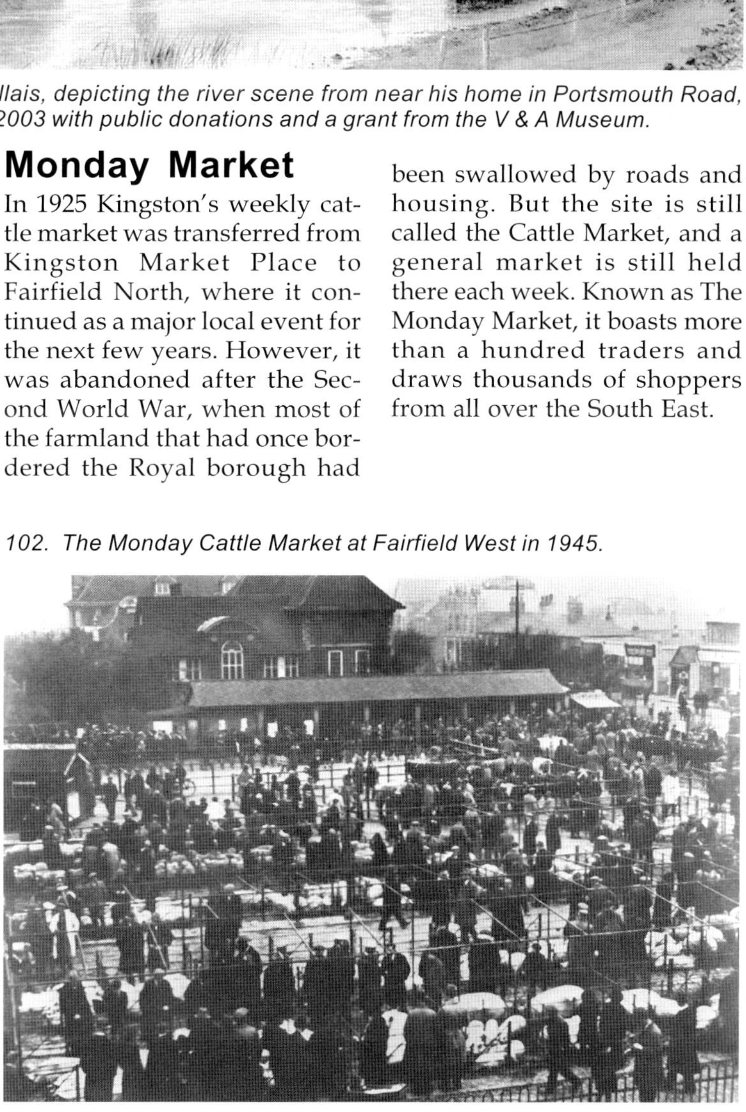

103. Eadweard Muybridge.

104. Eadweard Muybridge's 'Zoopraxiscope', the world's first 'movie projector' in effect. He bequeathed it to Kingston Museum.

Eadweard Muybridge

Muybridge (1830-1904) took the first accurate moving photographs, was progenitor of today's vast cinema industry and was notorious for most of his life. Yet Eadward Muybridge, one of the key innovators of the modern world, is a surprisingly low profile figure.

He was born Edward Muggeridge in Kingston and brought up at 30 High Street, where his father ran a coal and grain business on the ground floor and the family lived in the rooms above. He was educated at Kingston Grammar School, and a cousin remembered him as "an eccentric boy, rather mischievous, always doing something or saying something unusual, or inventing a new boy, a fresh trick." In 1851 he went to America, where he changed his surname to Muybridge.

After several missing years, during which he survived a serious coach crash, mastered the new art of photography and became one of the leading cameramen of the day, he began taking America by storm with his lecture tours, using the "zoopraxiscope" he had invented to show the first pictures of animals and humans in continuous motion. In 1872 he was able to show photographically that there was a moment in a horse's gallop when all four hooves were off the ground at once. He also made headlines when he murdered his wife's lover, was cleared by a sympathetic jury, and soon after returned from a foreign assignment to find his beautiful but faithless wife dead at 24.

By the time of his first public zoopraxiscope demonstration in England in 1882 he was a world celebrity. No-one had ever seen lifesize images of moving figures before and it caused a sensation. He also began spelling his name Eadweard inspired, it is said, by the names of the Saxon kings on the coronation stone of his home town of Kingston.

His triumph was marred by an act of vengeance, too long to detail here, by a powerful former patron determined to undermine achievements by claiming them as his own. Thomas Edison, the so-called inventor of cinematography, did exactly the same. True, Edison invented the kinetoscope. But he took his inspiration from the zoopraxiscope with which Muybridge gave America its first-ever public showing of moving photographs on 4 May, 1880.

"Mr Muybridge has laid the foundations of a new method of entertaining people...we predict it will make the round of the civilised world," reported the *Daily Alta California*, with remarkable accuracy.

Muybridge was content to let Edison take the credit for motion pictures, saying he wanted only to be remembered for his pioneering and hugely influential work with the zoopraxiscope. And he refused to have any truck with the movie industry, preferring academia to entertainment.

He spent the last 14 years of his life in Kingston, dying alone in 1904 in the garden of 2 Liverpool Road while building a scale model of the Great Lakes of North America. The house still survives, and a plaque in his memory was belatedly put on the garden wall in 1997. Another plaque was put on the front of his erstwhile family home by the Friends of Kingston Museum and Heritage in 2004 to mark the centenary of his death.

Knowing Kingston was about to have a new museum – it opened in the year he died – he bequeathed to it his zoopraxiscope, several boxes of discs, more than a thousand lantern slides and his personal scrapbook, with the request that they never leave the Royal borough. He also left a trust fund for the purchase of books, and an original of his famous 17-foot panorama of San Francisco, a spectacular technical feat which is still regarded as the greatest achievement of its kind. It is on permanent display in Kingston Museum, and is uniquely valuable as the only complete representation of the city before its destruction by an earthquake in 1906.

Muybridge's cremated remains were buried in Brookwood Cemetery, Woking beneath a brown slab which misspelled his name as Maybridge.

Napoleon III and Eugenie

It is difficult in history to find a more glamorous and dramatic couple than Napoleon III and Eugenie. He – officially the nephew of Napoleon Bonaparte, but thought to have been his son – had a life of extraordinary derring-do, attempting to win France by invading it from England in a single steamboat, escaping from life imprisonment in a fortress and eventually ruling France as Emperor for nearly two decades.

She was the beautiful

105. Napoleon III, depicted in September 1869.

106. Empress Eugenie in her later years as an exile, widow and bereaved mother.

daughter of a Spanish count, who held Napoleon's famously roving eye the moment he saw her galloping to the hunt in the Forest of Fontainbleu. They married in 1853, soon after he became Emperor, and together they dazzled the world during the heady years of the Second Empire.

Eugenie, cultured, charming and elegant, won all hearts, including Queen Victoria's. This in turn helped Napoleon to win international acclaim through a brilliant run of successes, including gaining Britain's support in the Crimean War, defeating the Austrians at Solferino and annexing Nice and Savoy.

What possible connection can this exotic couple have with Kingston Baptist Church, the sedate stone building that has stood in Union Street since 1864?

To answer that, one must look back to 1870, when Napoleon reluctantly led the French army into war against Prussia. It was a disastrous exercise. Less than two months later he was forced to surrender to the Germans at Sedan, his empire collapsed, and he was held captive until the war ended in 1871. Meanwhile Eugenie, who had ruled as regent while her husband was at the war front, had made a breathtaking escape from Parisian mobs roaring for her execution. She eventually reached Britain, where she set up home in Camden Place, a country house in Chislehurst. There she was joined by her only son, the Prince Imperial, and the following year her exiled husband.

One of his consolations in exile was an organ, built and installed in Camden Place by the eminent Victorian organ builder, T C Lewis. Its beautiful casework alone was an inspiration. Napoleon also took great pleasure in listening to the instrument and playing it.

His dream of recovering his lost empire was never fulfilled. He died at Camden Place from kidney disease in 1873.

The link with Kingston was forged in the 1890s, when Napoleon's church organ was transferred to Kingston Baptist church. It was a splendid part of worship there until the 1970s. Then age, a leaking roof and lack of repair funds made it unplayable.

An unremarkable electronic instrument was brought in as a substitute. Meanwhile the old instrument was put under wraps and virtually forgotten until 1998 when the minister, the Rev Roger Hoath, noticed a piece of wood protruding from a pile of old curtains and bric-a-brac. It was the pump lever of the organ.

After emergency first aid, organist Paul Zala coaxed a few notes from it while Mr Hoath laboriously pumped the blower. Since then restoration work has been carried out by Shepherd & Son, the Edgware organ builder, and the organ is again in regular use.

Postscript: After Napoleon's death, Eugenie lived at Coombe Cottage a country mansion which, converted into luxury apartments, still stands in Coombe Lane West. There she stayed in 1881-2, visited by Queen Victoria, and worshipped at St Raphael's Church in Portsmouth Road while a new home to replace Camden Place (which she hated) was prepared for her in Farnborough.

By then she had lost her son – killed while fighting with the British army in Zululand in 1879 – and was still in mourning. The *Surrey Comet* reported one of her sundry visits to St Raphael's:

> "The Empress looked careworn and sad, but pleasantly acknowledged the respect shown to her as she entered her carriage."

Queen Victoria, also in deep mourning, responded very differently to the public. As the *Comet* reported:

> "Her Majesty the Queen visited the Empress Eugenie at Coombe Cottage on Monday. Her Majesty alighted at Norbiton Station, where a closed carriage awaited her, and we were sorry to observe that Her Majesty manifested much nervousness and the whole arrangement was regulated with a cautious timidity which seemed almost a reflection upon the loy-

alty of the people. The windows of the royal carriage were drawn up immediately Her Majesty entered, and mounted attendants rode almost dangerously close, as if to hide from many loving eyes even a passing glance of our gracious Queen."

Newspapers

It might be an exaggeration to say that printers' ink was the lifeblood of Victorian Kingston, but it was certainly a staple ingredient. Printers operated throughout the town, pouring out the handbills, pamphlets, tickets, cards and posters so essential in a community before mass communication. There was also a proliferation of local journals. Anyone who felt specially roused over an issue, and had sufficient money, would launch his own newspaper as a vehicle for his pet topic until it had been resolved.

A typical example was the *Kingston Guardian*. Throughout 1899, and most of 1900, the great local talking point was the imminent replacement of horse-drawn omnibuses by electrically driven tramcars. The idea came from America, and one half of the town was convinced that the new enterprise should be run by the American-sponsored London United Tramways while the other half felt that such an important project, involving the demolition of much of the town centre to allow for road widening, should be in the hands of Kingston Council. Tempers had reached white heat when the United Tramways' managing director, Sir Clifton Robinson, decided to win public support by launching his own newspaper. The news content was meagre; its main content was propaganda extolling the efficiency and thrift of London United Tramways.

It was too much for a loyal local patriot called Thomas Guilford. He fired back with *The Kingston Guardian*, a zippy little newspaper produced from his printing works in Wood Street, and dedicated to fighting the corporation's case. Finally, in 1900, a local election was held to settle the issue. In a poll ruined by hundreds of

107. The composing room of the Surrey Comet *in 1909.*

108. The Surrey Comet's *home in 1888, formerly a butcher's shop and slaughter house.*

spoiled voting papers, on which electors had simply scrawled "No Trams", London United Tramways finally won the day. Sir Clifton savoured his triumph by moving into the handsome Garrick's Villa at Hampton and having his own private electric tramway brought to his front door.

A brave attempt to topple the establishment was made by William Tye in the 1880s with his *Kingston Reformer*. This beautifully printed newspaper was produced at Park Road, Kingston Hill, but was too much against mainstream public opinion to survive for long. However, it did prepare the way for the *Kingston Express*, launched by Eaton Hart of St James's Road during the Parliamentary elections of 1882 as "the biggest halfpenny newspaper in the country."

Both William Drewett, with his *Kingston and Surbiton News* and the Knapp family, owners of the *Surrey Comet*, were dedicated to the Conservative candidate, Sir Richard Temple, and used their papers to abuse the Liberal contender, Charles Hodgson, in scathing terms. So the staunchly Liberal Eaton Hart set up a rival paper to champion Mr Hodgson. He failed in the elections, but the *Kingston Express*, and later the *Kingston Guardian*, made local history by demonstrating for the first time how newspaper warfare could dent the status quo in the town.

But the most important printing event in 19th century Kingston was the introduction of the *Surrey Comet* in 1854. Its owner was Thomas Philpott, a devout Christian who felt God was calling him to launch a newspaper that would "promote the good and expose the bad." The first issue was a modest four-page effort, measuring only 13.5 inches long by 8.5 inches wide, and until failing health forced Philpott to retire in 1859 it was edited, printed and published from his printing and stationery business in Surbiton.

The *Comet* was then bought by Russell Knapp, and transferred to Kingston. He died suddenly in 1867 at the age of 36, leaving his wife, Mary Anne with eight children, including twins born a month after the death of their father. Courageously she took control of her husband's business, and ran it as sole proprietor for 33 years.

The *Comet* was independently owned until 1982, when it was acquired by Argus Press, a subsidiary of BET. In 1993 it was bought by Reed Regional Newspapers and subsequently by Newsquest, the UK's second largest publisher of provincial and local newspapers, and a subsidiary of the American owned Gannett company. It is still going strong, and is now the oldest surviving newspaper in Surrey.

The *Kingston and Surbiton News*, founded in 1881, lasted until 1900, when it amalgamated with the *Comet*.

Nipper

In 1895 an aggressive little terrier called Nipper suffered a stroke, died and was buried beneath a mulberry tree in the garden of 77 Clarence Street, Kingston. He was, it seems, the terror of all neighbouring dogs

109. The celebrated His Master's Voice logo, featuring Nipper.

110. Clarence Street in 1895, looking west towards Kingston Bridge. Nipper, the HMV dog, lived here in the premises just beyond the Livery & Bait stables. A few years after this photograph, tramlines were installed and several buildings at the western end were demolished for road widening.

and loved illicitly hunting pheasants in Richmond Park. A few years later, against all the odds, he became the most famous dog in the world when a painting of him became the trademark of The Gramophone Company, and was used on all the records and other merchandise issued world-wide under His Master's Voice label.

Nipper is believed to have been born in 1884 and was first owned by Mark Henry Barraud, a theatre scenery artist in Bristol. When Mark died, Nipper passed to his brother Francis (1856-1924), who was also an artist (they were the sons of painter Henry Barraud). Later, in an undated note, Francis described how "it suddenly occurred to me that to have my dog listening to the phonograph, with an intelligent and rather puzzled expression, and call it His Master's Voice, would make an excellent subject. We had a phonograph, and I often noticed how puzzled he was to make out where the voice came from. It was certainly the happiest thought I ever had."

111. The plaque erected by HMV in memory of Nipper in 1984.

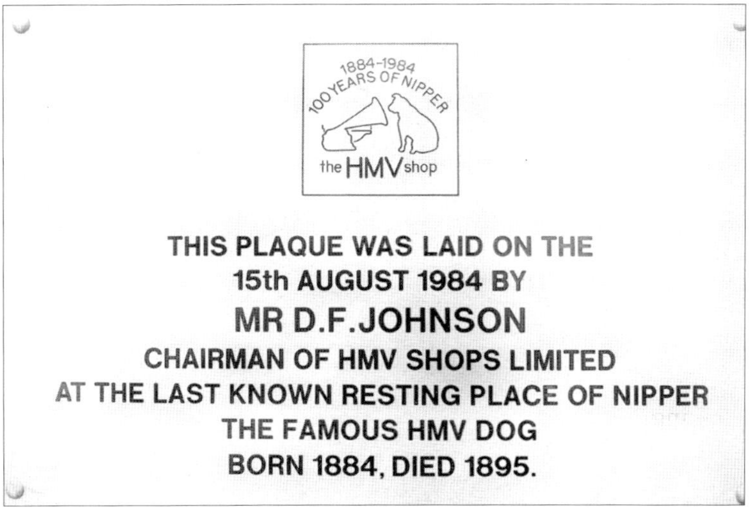

Eventually, in 1899, The Gramophone Company bought the picture for £100 (including the copyright), on condition Barraud replaced the phonograph with a gramophone. Nipper made his debut on the company's advertising literature in 1900 and on gramophone records in 1909. By December 1910 he was appearing on all the company's products.

In 1984, to mark the centenary of Nipper's birth, the chairman of HMV shops, David Johnson, laid a plaque on the dog's last resting place. By then the erstwhile garden had become a car park owned by Lloyds Bank, and the plaque was so damaged by cars that a replacement was placed on a nearby wall.

Oxfam Shop, 30 London Road

Against all the odds, and many perilous near misses, this building managed to survive the sweeping re-developments of the 19th and 20th centuries. It is fortunate it did, for it has a unique place in Kingston's pub and building history.

It began life more than 300 years ago as The Three Coneys, a country alehouse surrounded by farmland and orchards. At that time large areas of Kingston were being rebuilt or embellished with bricks - then a revolutionary new medium for domestic buildings. Local hand-made field bricks, probably from Kingston's earliest known brickworks in the wilds of what is now Cambridge Road, were used for The Three Coneys. They are multi-coloured and irregular in size and, by modern standards, ex-

112. The Oxfam shop in London Road, a listed building marred by a modern shop fascia and on-street parking.

tremely crude. At the time the alehouse was built, however, they would have been the last word in modern construction.

The same bricks were used to build Cleave's Almshouses on the opposite side of the road, indicating that the two buildings were put up at about the same time, i.e during the 1660s. This part of Norbiton was where many of Kingston's earliest bricklayers lived, and the Three Coneys itself seems to have been occupied by bricklayers from the moment it was built. The earliest tenants were the Pearsons, who were master bricklayers in the town from at least the early 1600s, and succeeding generations of the family seem to have lived there until it ceased to be an alehouse in the 18th century.

Bricks, once an important local product, were the best thing that ever happened to pub profits in Kingston. Both the making and the laying of them was a cruelly dusty and parching occupation, made physically possible only by frequent visits to the nearest alehouse for refreshment. Thus it is no coincidence that The Three Coneys should have been tenanted and run by a bricklaying family.

But what makes this former pub of special interest today is that it is almost certainly the oldest brick house left in Kingston.

The gruelling life of a bricklayer in old Kingston is vividly portrayed in *The Bricklayers Miscellany*, a collection of poems by Robert Tatersal, published in 1734.

"I hope these poetical performances of a country bricklayer may...meet in the worlde some favourable reception," wrote Tatersal in his sixpenny volume.

It was not to be. He continued to live in impoverished obscurity in Kingston's Thames Street. But his poem, *To Bricklayers Labours*, describes a typical day in the life of a Kingston bricklayer some 270 years ago. It also explains why local pubs opened at dawn - a practice continued until comparatively recent times:

"Hanging on my Threadbare Coat and Hose,
My Hat, my Cap, my Breeches and my Shoes;
with Sheep-skin Apron girt about my Waste,
Down Stairs I go to visit my Repast;
Which rarely doth consist of more than these,
A Quartern Loaf and Half a Pound of Cheese.
Then in a Linnen Bag, on purpose made,
My Day's Allowance o're my Shoulder laid;
And first, to keep the Fog from coming in,

I whet my Whistle with a Dram of Gin.
So thus equipped, my Trowl in my hand,
I haste to Work and join the ragged Band;
And now each one his different Post assigned
And three in three in Ranks completely joined."

Tatersal describes the sweated labour of the morning. Then, after slaking their frantic thirst with lunch-time ale:

Again we reassume the dusty Stage,
The Mortar chaf'd again we do engage;
This the most tedious part of all the Day
Full five Hours space to toil without Allay;
Now parch'd with Heat and almost chok'd with Dust,
We join our pence to satiate our Thirst..."

Parking

In 1925 Kingston Council built its first 'public motor park'. Resembling an aircraft hangar, and occupying a site previously covered by old shops on the west side of Eden Street, its aim was "to reduce the congestion of stationary cars in the streets" by offering all-day parking for 6d (2.5p). It proved so popular that the following year it was extended by 100 spaces.

The council vowed that the new amenity would not put an end to street parking.

"No-one wants to drive trade away, and no-one could cavil at a car stopping in the Market Place for half-an-hour or so," said a spokesman.

Leonard Bentall provided Kingston's second car park in 1928. Money was tight at the time, and he realised that as customers were spending less, he must attract many more of them. A new covered car park would, he decided, bring in people from far beyond Kingston, especially if there was also a luxurious new restaurant on hand for them when they got there.

The result was Bentalls Tudor Restaurant and an indoor park for 450 cars on land previously covered by eight cottages and the riverside mansion, Down Hall. The park was an instant success, with a turnover of more than a thousand vehicles on Saturdays. But it was another 30 years before the old freedoms began to disappear, and parking became a major local issue.

In October 1962 parking meters were introduced in the town centre, allowing a maximum of two hours at 6d an hour. Those who went over that time risked a summons and an

113. The American architect Howard Crane designed a multi-storey car park (seen here) for Bentalls in 1946, incorporating a garage, petrol station and restaurant. The idea was shelved until 1969, when the plan formed the basis of a new car park that was topped out by the Minister of Transport, Ernest Marples on 21 November. It was demolished to make way for a larger park to serve the new Bentall Centre.

excess charge of 10s (50p). Over the next few months there was such an avalanche of summonses that special courts were set up to deal with them. Nevertheless, the hated machines reduced jams caused by cars parked on both sides of the road, and also forced all-day kerb hogs to use car parks.

This made more facilities essential. By Christmas 1962 there was space for 200 cars on land acquired by the council from the South East Gas Board in Lower Ham Road. Sixty more spaces were created in 1965 by demolishing the retort house and other buildings used by the gasworks before its closure in 1955. Charges were 6d for the first two hours, and 6d for each additional hour.

Meanwhile Alderman A G Knowldon's idea of an underground car park at the Fairfield was vetoed because of the proximity of the river and the cost of making it watertight. But it became a reality 25 years later when the Cattle Market park opened with 491 underground spaces.

In 1963 temporary parks were set up on Alliance Property Group's development site in Fairfield West, and the former Gaze's site, bounded by High Street and Kingston Hall Road. And in November that year meter zones were extended beyond the town centre, with a charge of a shilling (5p) for the first four hours.

A new chapter in local parking history was Kingston's first multi-storey park, officially opened by the Earl of Westmoreland at Eden Walk in 1966. It cost £875,000, had 550 spaces and replaced the corporation's original park in Eden

114. The Earl of Westmoreland opening the multi-storey car park in Eden Street, October 1966.

Street. But still parking provisions were woefully inadequate. So, after long negotiation with no fewer than 14 unenthusiastic council committees, Bentall's opened a multi-storey park for 750 cars in 1969. This, a showpiece of its time, was demolished and replaced by a larger multi-storey to provide parking both for a re-modelled Bentall's store, which opened in 1990, and the Bentall Centre, which opened two years later.

Another multi-storey car park, Draper's, opened in Kingston Hall Road in 1982 with 400 spaces, followed by a fourth with 813 spaces in The Bittoms. The latest multi-storey is Seven Kings, opened in Skerne Road in 2002 with 700 spaces.

Cesar Picton

For more than a century after his death, he was a forgotten man. Now he is an icon for Kingston Racial Equality Council, and there is a Picton Trust and a Cesar Picton Lecture named in his memory.

The story begins in the 1760s, when Britain was at war with France on the west coast of Africa. Serving with the British forces was a disgruntled Captain John Parr, who in 1761 resigned his commission and returned to Britain, bringing with him a six-year-old black boy as a gift for his friend, Sir John Philipps, of Norbiton Place, Kingston. This was a mansion that stood in parkland near today's Coombe Road/London Road junction. Richly dressed black pageboys were fashionable in aristocratic households then and accounts show the newcomer received new clothes and "a velvet turbet." He was also given a Christian baptism and the name Cesar – one of the classical names much in vogue at that time. In later life he added the surname Picton after Picton Castle, the Philipps' family seat since Norman times.

There is a misconception that Cesar was a 'slave', who overcame servitude to become a man of property. In fact, he was the special protégé of Lady Philipps and, like all upper staff in aristocratic household, enjoyed a high standard of living and a comfortable income. He also seems to have mixed on virtually equal terms with the family, which had a long tradition of supporting education and Christian missionary work.

For the next 27 years he divided his time between Norbiton Place and Picton Castle. Sir John was often away on political and charitable work, and Cesar became a firm favourite of Lady Philipps and her three unmarried daughters. Sir John died in 1764, leaving Norbiton Place to his wife for life, and then to their only son, Lord Milford. So it was known that when Lady Philipps died, the old way of life must end.

Lady Philipps eventually died in 1788, and Lord Milford sold Norbiton Place soon after her burial in Kingston parish church. She left Cesar £100, a considerable sum at that time, which enabled him to rent, and subsequently buy, a riverside house in Kingston's West-by-Thames (later renamed High Street) and begin a new career as a coal merchant. Later he received further legacies of £250, plus a £30 life annuity, from the three Philipps daughters.

He chose to specialise in coal because the Philipps family owned coalpits and took an active interest in them, so Cesar had good knowledge of the trade. Years in an aristocratic household had also given him the style and polish to socialise easily, and eventually achieve his aim of becoming a 'gentleman', i.e. a man wealthy enough to live well without paid work. He proved to have a keen business acumen, increasing his profits until, in 1795, he could buy his Kingston premises.

He named them Picton House, and they are described in rating assessments as "house, buildings, wharf, garden, yard and buildings opposite" (the latter became famous as the Old Malt House, a much-loved historic landmark illegally destroyed in the 1960s).

By 1807 he could retire and live on his rents and capital as "Cesar Picton of Tolworth, gentleman". Further proof of his commercial success is that in 1816 he bought an estate at Thames Ditton for the then huge sum of £4,000 without raising a mortgage or selling his properties in Kingston and Tolworth. He named his new home Picton House, and here he lived for the rest of his life, always elegantly dressed, and keeping a smart horse and chaise.

He died in 1836. In his will he asks to be "plain but decently buried within the Parish Church of Kingston" and that mourning rings, costing no more than £5 each, be distributed to sixteen named friends. His wishes were obeyed, and his last resting place in Kingston parish church is marked by a floor plaque in the south aisle inscribed 'CP 1836'. His existence was eventually forgotten, and would have remained so had not Kingston upon Thames Archaeological Society begun intensive research on Kingston's Picton House in the 1970s, during a successful campaign to save it from demolition. That research, involving years of sifting through rate assessments, wills, deeds and other archives, led to the re-discovery of Cesar and his unique story.

An interesting aspect of the Cesar saga is that his colour seems never to have been an issue. He had innumerable friends, the respect of the business community, and took an active part in charitable and local affairs. The only reference to his race is a note pencilled in the margin of an old book owned by Kingston Museum and Heritage Service. It reads: "Cesar Picton was a man of colour and immense bulk and had to be brought to the church for interment on a four-wheel trolley and laid into the vault down an inclined plane of planks on rollers. Four coffins had to be adapted to make his coffin."

Pre-Raphaelites

It cannot be claimed that Pre-Raphaelite art was actually born in Kingston. But this movement, which was to influence art on an international scale, had roots in the Royal borough, and in the unspoilt countryside which surrounded it at that time.

John Everett Millais, the mainspring of the original Pre-Raphaelite Brotherhood, lived with his parents in Kingston and painted many of his early pictures there. The family lived in South Cottage, which stood close to the spot now occupied by the TA Centre in Portsmouth Road. The household comprised John William Millais, his wife Emily, and their two sons John and William. They had come to the London area from Jersey to further John's art education; for he had been a child prodigy, en-

115. *'My First Sermon' (1862/3) by John Everett Millais. It shows his daughter Effie in a high-backed pew at Kingston parish church.*

tering the Royal Academy schools at 11 and exhibiting at the Royal Academy from the age of 27. A hayloft at South Cottage was converted into a studio for young John, and here he produced several of his early works.

William Ayliffe, who recounted his "memories of an octogenarian" to the *Surrey Comet* in 1914, knew the family well. He recalled the father, John William Millais, as "a very tall, fine-looking man," who frequently brought his son to his photographic studio in the town centre. Here Ayliffe photographed many figures for the young artist's studies, usually children from a local private school.

The seeds of Pre-Raphaelism were sown when Millais visited a close family friend in the countryside between Kingston and Ewell. At the same time artist Holman Hunt was staying with relatives at Rectory Farm, Ewell. The two found they had kindred artistic ideals and the result was the Pre-Raphaelite Brotherhood, the secret society of seven artists with they founded in 1848, when Millais was 19 and Hunt 24.

Initially Millais and Hunt lodged at Laburnham Cottage, next to the Victoria Inn in Ewell Road, Surbiton, going out daily to the Hogsmill River to paint their respective pictures.

Public Lavatories

A major talking point in Kingston in 1897 was the opening of the first public lavatory for ladies. There had long been a few crude facilities for men – the 17th-century Kingston Chamberlain's accounts refer to four shillings "paid to John Brown for mending the pissing place under Court Hall" – but nothing at all for women. An official report in the 19th century highlighted "the sufferings which must be endured by all, but more especially by females, on account of the want of public conveniences."

Those that did exist were described as "plague spots that are offensive to the eye and a reproach to the metropolis." But the subject was considered indelicate, and in Kingston nothing was done until 1897, when the council decided to convert the former bath house in Bath Passage into public lavatories, with separate sections for ladies and gentlemen.

There was some dissent. One councillor pointed out that the building was close to the Assize Courts "where people not of the greatest refinement are in the habit of congregating." It was also near a slaughterhouse and ladies, he felt sure, "would not like to go there." Another councillor objected on the grounds that a men's lavatory, built in nearby High Street for £137, had taken only £12 in a year. For those were the days when 'halting stations', as they were known, were expected to be self-supporting, and people really did 'spend a penny' to use them.

Eventually the old bath house *was* converted, and its facilities proved so popular that when it was demolished in 1933 to make way for the present Guildhall, replacement lavatories were built a few yards away, where they have remained ever since.

Public Houses

It began as a gentle breeze, unnoticed by the public at large, when the Monopolies and Mergers Commission (MMC) took a close look at British brewing in the early 1980s. It swelled to a wind when the government issued Beer Orders in 1989. and it became a hurricane from 1992 when those orders, based on the MMC's findings, came into effect. Since then more than 25% of UK pubs have changed hands, or closed, or been altered beyond recognition in the biggest upheaval ever in Britain's long history of innkeeping.

The Beer Orders were intended to loosen the grip of the big five breweries: Bass, Courage/Grand Met, Allied, Whitbread and Scottish Newcastle, who at that time controlled 67% of the pub beer market through their huge estates of tied houses, where only their beers could be sold. They also had 17,500 'free' houses in thrall by giving publicans low-interest trade loans if they operated a tie. The result was a monopoly which kept smaller breweries in the cold, restricted customers' choice, kept prices high, and put tenants in a poor bargaining position. Hence the Beer Orders, which decreed that by 1 November 1992 brewers owning more than 2,000 on-licensed premises must either give up brewing or release from tie half their pubs above the 2,000 limit.

Many factors, notably a recession and canny regrouping by the big breweries, stopped the Beer Orders achieving the intended Utopia. But they gave birth to a new breed of independent operators who made big, sometimes controversial changes.

One of the first to scent the future turn of events was J D Wetherspoon. This was founded by lawyer Tim Martin (and named after one of his schoolmasters) in 1979 when be bought - and later sold - the Kingston Mill in the High Street. However, his main aim was to create new hostelries in previously unlicensed buildings. A prime example of this policy is Kingston's former Empire Theatre in Clarence Street, which became a Wetherspoon's pub, the King's Tun, in 1997. By the spring of 2006 there were some 660 Wetherspoon pubs, with more in the pipeline.

Beer Orders were not the only reason for radical changes in Kingston's public house scene. The construction of a new relief road *(qv)*, plus the demand for more commercial property development, also played their part in a 'musical

116 and 117. Two pubs demolished to make way for the relief road. Above, the Kingston Hotel in Clarence Street and below, the Royal Charter in Richmond Road.

118. A pub built in the 1860s to serve passengers at the new railway station opposite. It was renamed the Artful Dodger in the 1980s.

119. The Griffin before conversion.

chairs' situation in which buildings that had always been pubs were demolished or converted into something else while buildings that had always been something else became pubs!

Victims of the relief road included the Kingston Hotel, an imposing structure built immediately opposite Kingston Station in 1879; The Castle, which opened in 1897 on the corner of Fairfield Road and Fairfield West (later renamed Lady Booth Road and Wheatfield Road respectively); The Jolly Brewer, which evolved from a tiny Victorian beerhouse in Canbury Passage; and The Royal Charter (formerly The Three Fishes) in Richmond Road.

The most prominent example of licensed premises giving way to commercial redevelopment was The Griffin, established in Kingston Market Place in the reign of Henry VIII, rebuilt in the reign of Charles II, refronted in Victoria's reign and 'improved' in each of the four reigns (excluding that of Edward VIII) of the 20th century. Throughout its life it was popularly known as "the headquarters of Kingston", where most of the major meetings and social functions of the town took place. However, this long history ended abruptly at the start of 1985 when The Griffin closed without warning. The only public notice was the word "closed" scrawled in chalk on the locked doors.

It transpired that the building had been bought by Hilstone Developments, who sold it to Historic City Developments a year later. In late 1987 it began a new career as a shopping centre. The only period features to be retained were the frontage and the fine Victorian ballroom on the first floor – now a restaurant.

Also seduced by commercial developers was The Old Crown in Church Street. This was the oldest pub in Kingston, with a history stretching back at least to 1417, when it was called The Chequer. It was rebuilt in the 17th century, and given a new brick frontage in the 18th. It was variously known as The Horse & Groom, The Crown and the Bull & Butcher, until becoming

120. *The Jolly Brewer, demolished for the relief road.*

122. *The Druid's Head.*

The Old Crown from the early 19th century until it was converted into two shops in 1984. However, its 17th-century structure was retained virtually intact on the upper floor.

Meanwhile the Row Barge ended its long tenure in Old Bridge Street when it was demolished to make way for the new John Lewis store, which opened in 1990. The Three Compasses in Eden Street, reputed to be 400 years old when it was demolished in 1906 and replaced by a new building, was in turn taken down in 1977 for the second stage of the Eden Walk Shopping Mall. The pub derived its name from the arms of the Carpenters' Company, whose craftsmen were a flourishing part of Kingston's economy from the 14th century.

The Three Horseshoes in Eden Street disappeared in 1971, together with the former Kingston Brewery which adjoined it, to make way for shops, a multi-storey car park and new headquarters for Lever Brothers. It was replaced in 1975 by a circular, heptagon-shaped pub called the Seven Saxons. but this closed within a few years and became a branch of the Cheltenham & Gloucester Building Society. On the other hand, the Midland Bank at 43 Market Place became a pub, The Financier and Firkin, in the 1990s. When that closed later in the decade it was converted into a restaurant.

Once upon a time Kingston Market Place had 13 pubs – now it has only one, The Druid's Head. This was extensively refurbished by Whitbread's in 1992, who also doubled its size by extending into the former restaurant next door. At odds with the modern ground floor in the original building is a fine 17th-century staircase leading to the well-preserved Stuart rooms on the upper floor. This pub, a favourite of Jerome K Jerome, was The Lion and Lamb until the 19th century, when it was renamed by a landlord who was a noted member of The Ancient Order of Druids.

As old pubs have gone from the town centre, new ones have arisen. One of the first was The Bishop Out of Residence, built on the riverside near Kingston Bridge in the early 1980s. Another, opened further up-river in 1982, was The Gazebo. Further downstream, in Canbury Gardens, a former restaurant was coverted into the riverside pub, Boaters.

Modern-style bars have done much to woo younger customers from traditional pubs. Prime examples are Casa and Ha Ha Bar, both in the Charter Quay development that was

121. *The Bishop out of Residence, a pub of the late 20th century.*

123. Wood Street as it was until the 1980s.

completed in 2003. Another is Porter Blacks, formerly Punters, which has been a feature of the river front behind High Street since the 1980s.

The Relief Road

Nothing had greater impact on central Kingston in the 20th century than the relief road, both in terms of the dismal planning blight that preceded it and the sweeping changes needed to accomplish it.

The road was central to the Kingston Town Centre Development Plan, unveiled in 1963. Surrey County Council and Kingston Council had privately formed the scheme for more than two years; but when it was finally unveiled, only a few weeks were allowed for public comments. The result was a furious outcry, and the decision by Kingston Chamber of Commerce to embark on its costliest exercise ever: opposing the plan at a public inquiry and commissioning an alternative scheme.

The council plan involved mass demolition of shops, offices, cinemas, pubs and houses, with powers of compulsory acquisition if owners objected. Twenty-one areas would be subject to compulsory purchase, including 19 acres of the town centre, bounded by Wood Street and Cromwell Road in the north, Fairfield Road and London Road in the south, and parts of Fife Road and Clarence Street. Also earmarked were six acres between the river and Wood Street, plus more than three acres bounded by London Road, Coombe Road and the railway – needed for the junction of a massive east-west throughway. This was to be taken on a raised flyover, soaring above a major roundabout near Kingston Station before leading traffic to a second Thames bridge to be built north of the present one. There would also be a north-south throughway, plus a ring road running along the river bank south of Kingston Bridge.

Several historic buildings would have to go, including Kingston Baptist church, Kingston Museum and Kingston Central Library. The £30 million scheme would take 20 years to construct, and make the town centre a motorway-enclosed island.

The Chamber fought the plan with all its might, taking days to present its case. It paid a heavy price. The cost of legal and professional fees, plus

124. An example by the riverside of the planning blight that afflicted Kingston in the 1960s-70s, waiting for decisions on the relief road.

conflicting with the council head-on, put it deep in debt, and marred relations with the Guildhall for years to come.

Meanwhile the Kingston Society was founded in 1962 to fight the riverside road proposals that would have ruined one of the town's finest assets and, in the society's words, form "an avoidable physical and psychological barrier between the living and working body of the town and its lungs and eyes."

As it happened, the controversial scheme never materialised. Repudiated by the Greater London Council (GLC), which took responsibility for metropolitan roads after 1965, it was scrapped in 1974. It was victory of a sort. But Kingston businesses then had to contend with continuing planning blight while the council and the GLC formed new proposals. Thus the Horsefair remained a derelict waste and Thames Street, once noted as 'the Bond Street of Surrey', withered still further under the threat of compulsory purchase orders. So did Eden Street and the river front, which degenerated into decayed sites and remnants of past industries, including the former Eagle Brewery, Palmer's seacoal wharves and the burnt-out ruins of Kingston Tannery. It was increasingly difficult to laud crumbling, traffic-choked Kingston as a destination town until a new road scheme was approved in 1981 and completed in 1989. Its construction, helped along by the £20 million which the council managed to win from the GLC before its demise, involved the loss of many familiar features and resulted, among other things, in the diversion of all traffic round a new dual-carriageway loop and the pedestrianisation of Clarence Street, previously one of the busiest streets in Surrey. But it was far less destructive of the townscape than the first plan had been.

125. Wood Street after the completion of the relief road.

Lord Ripon

Lord Ripon, owner of Kingston's stateliest mansion, was the worst bore, and the finest shot, in English high society. He earned the first distinction by being devoid of humour, wit or conversation, and the second by shooting at least 556,813 head of game. Indeed, he was holding a gun when he dropped dead in 1923 after bagging 52 grouse.

Lord Ripon, born in 1852, became Earl de Grey when his father was created Marquess of Ripon in 1871. He had few of his father's qualities. The 1st Marquess was Viceroy of India and a statesman of rare integrity. But his only son – who became Lord Ripon after succeeding his father as 2nd Marquess in 1909 - had no interests beyond shooting, which he started in 1867, and made his lifelong obsession.

In 1886 he paused briefly from shooting to marry Gladys Lonsdale *(qv Gladys de Grey)*, an irrepressibly merry widow described by the then Prince of Wales as "a professional beauty." She had so many ardent admirers that society was taken aback when she announced her engagement to the taciturn Lord de Grey. She told a friend it was because he offered her "peace and comfort" A more accurate reason might be that he was heir to a marquessate and 24,000 acres, and his wealth and preoccupation with guns would leave her free to continue her reign as the lively queen of late 19th and early 20th century society.

The newly-weds bought Coombe Warren, a house built on Kingston Hill 17 years previously by John Galsworthy, father of the author. Gladys renamed it Coombe Court, and extended it on a massive scale, virtually doubling the accommodation and adding a concert hall and ballroom.

She was a close friend of Edward VII and Queen Alexandra, and the chief patron of the London opera and ballet seasons. Consequently her parties at Coombe Court were among the most brilliant in Britain.

Gladys died in 1917, leaving her husband in lonely splendour at Coombe Court with a butler and large staff to attend him. When he died, the house passed to Lady Juliet Duff, Gladys's only child by her first marriage to the Earl of Lonsdale.

The mansion was demolished in 1931, but its original entrance and lodge, and much of its landscaping, still survive in George Road.

The Riverside Walk

Kingston's greatest environmental achievement of the 20th century is the riverside walk, a beautiful public promenade that follows a 1.2 mile stretch of the Thames, and took 147 years to accomplish.

The Victorians made a start with the opening of Queen's Promenade at the southern end

126. Coombe Court, home of the Marquis of Ripon.

of the waterfront in 1856, followed by Canbury Gardens at the northern end in 1890. But the long stretch in between was given over to industries that needed the river. These included three boat-building works (Turk's, Eastland's and Burgoine's); Gridley Miskin's timber works; Kingston Tannery; the Eagle Brewery; Salter's Steamers; and Palmer's the seacoal specialists, who operated from the Pioneer and Eagle Wharves.

The final stretch before reaching Queen's Promenade was Town End Wharf, which for centuries had offered public facilities for the landing and despatch of commercial cargoes to and from the town's fac-

128. Buckland's Wharf and Thames Side in the 1980s. Every building has since gone. The electricity power station in the background was demolished in 1994 and replaced by a residential estate.

127. At the riverside. Every building in this picture has gone, including the power station with its lofty chimneys and Bentall's car park (right background). Gridley Miskin's timber yard was a major feature here from 1845 to 1982. It moved to the other side of the river because the town centre relief road was originally planned to run alongside the river. Beyond the timber yard is Turk's boatyard (qv).

tories and workshops.

These disappeared over time, and the task of uniting their disparate plots into a public walkway was mooted as far back as 1946, when it was also planned to build in Canbury Gardens a theatre and an open-air lido, with water heated by surplus steam from the new power station that was nearing completion nearby. However, arguments over land ownership, funding, and other issues dragged on for years.

A small start was made in 1961 when Queen's Promenade was lengthened to the north. But major progress was first achieved in 1974, when the promenade was extended right along Town End Wharf. Then, in 1975, came the opening up of Eagle Wharf. The next step forward occurred in 1979, with the building of a landscaped river promenade, plus Bishops Palace House and the Bishop Out of Residence pub on the site of the old tannery (which had burnt down in 1963). This was followed in 1982 with the creation of the Gazebo pub, giving the riverside walk a continuous length from Kingston Bridge to King's Passage.

Another missing link was forged in 1984/5, with the extension of the path from Forge House at the top of High Street to Eagle Wharf. Another coup came in 1990 with the creation on part of the former Gridley Miskin site of a riverside walk extending from Kingston Bridge to Vicarage Road (18 years previously Gridley Miskin, whose laden barges and lofty storage were long a familiar feature of the river, had had to leave Kingston after 106 years, and concentrate activities on its Hampton Wick wharf, when Kingston council acquired its site for a riverside relief road that, thankfully, never materialised).

That left one short gap until, after a 12-year delay, work began on the Charter Quay scheme. That was completed in 2003, and with it an uninterrupted riverside walk that is one of Kingston's major assets.

The Rotunda

One of the first 21st-century changes to Kingston's central townscape was the creation of the Rotunda on what had been Kingston bus station and Bentalls furniture depository.

The idea for the Rotunda was conceived by Clearwater Estates in 1996, when they learned that Bentalls wanted to dispose of its famous depository, a landmark building modelled on a Spanish palace. They beat off fierce competition from four other firms to secure it. Then, because the depository is a listed monument, there were protracted talks with English Heritage, plus complex negotiations to acquire adjoining sites. By the end of 1997 all these issues had been settled but, through was what described as Kingston Council's "negativity", construction did not begin until January 2000 – the year Clearwater had hoped to have it finished. It was completed in October 2002.

The complex was designed by local architects PRC Fewster of Surbiton. At its core is the depository, elegantly restored outside, and skilfully converted inside to provide a 14-screen Odeon cinema, with the boiler and other plant installed in the depository's central tower. The rest of the Rotunda, so named because of the curved glass tower on its centre front, is occupied by restaurants and a health club.

Royal Charters

April 26, 2000 was an anniversary of major local importance because it was 800 years to the day since King John granted Kingston its first recorded charter. This piece of parchment, which cost the townspeople six

129. The site of the Rotunda. Pine World was housed in one of the town's early cinemas. Adjoining it is the bus station, dating from the 1920s. Beyond that is the Granada, later extensively rebuilt as the night club Oceana.

130. The Rotunda, opened in 2002.

marks, and has long since disappeared, was of crucial significance because it marked the birth of Kingston as a town. Previous to that it had been an elaborate Royal farm and administrative centre.

King John granted the charter following petitions from Kingstonians eager to sample self-government. Its key was that, for the first time, it allowed Kingston to collect its own "fee farm rent" - the annual revenue due to the Crown - and pay it direct to the Exchequer. Previously these royal dues had been collected by the county sheriff, who was appointed to act as the King's agent and run local affairs, and often extorted more than was owed to line his own pockets.

Thanks to archaeological discoveries in 1999, it is now known that, after many centuries as a riverside village, Kingston was laid out as a 'new town' around 1170. Its main components were the Market Place and four bridges - two of which survive - and it is clear that, having transformed itself into a town physically, it was anxious to win recognition of the fact legally.

The new privileges were confirmed in a second charter from King John in 1208. This, the oldest document in Kingston Borough Archives, gives "to all our free men of Kingston our town of Kingston...to them and their heirs...for ever...and we will that neither the sheriff nor his bailiffs shall meddle in anything concerning the said town."

Kingston has been granted 30 more charters since then. The more notable ones include the Charter of Incorporation, granted by Edward IV in 1481

131. Kingston's Charter of Incorporation from Edward IV, dated 26 February 1481.

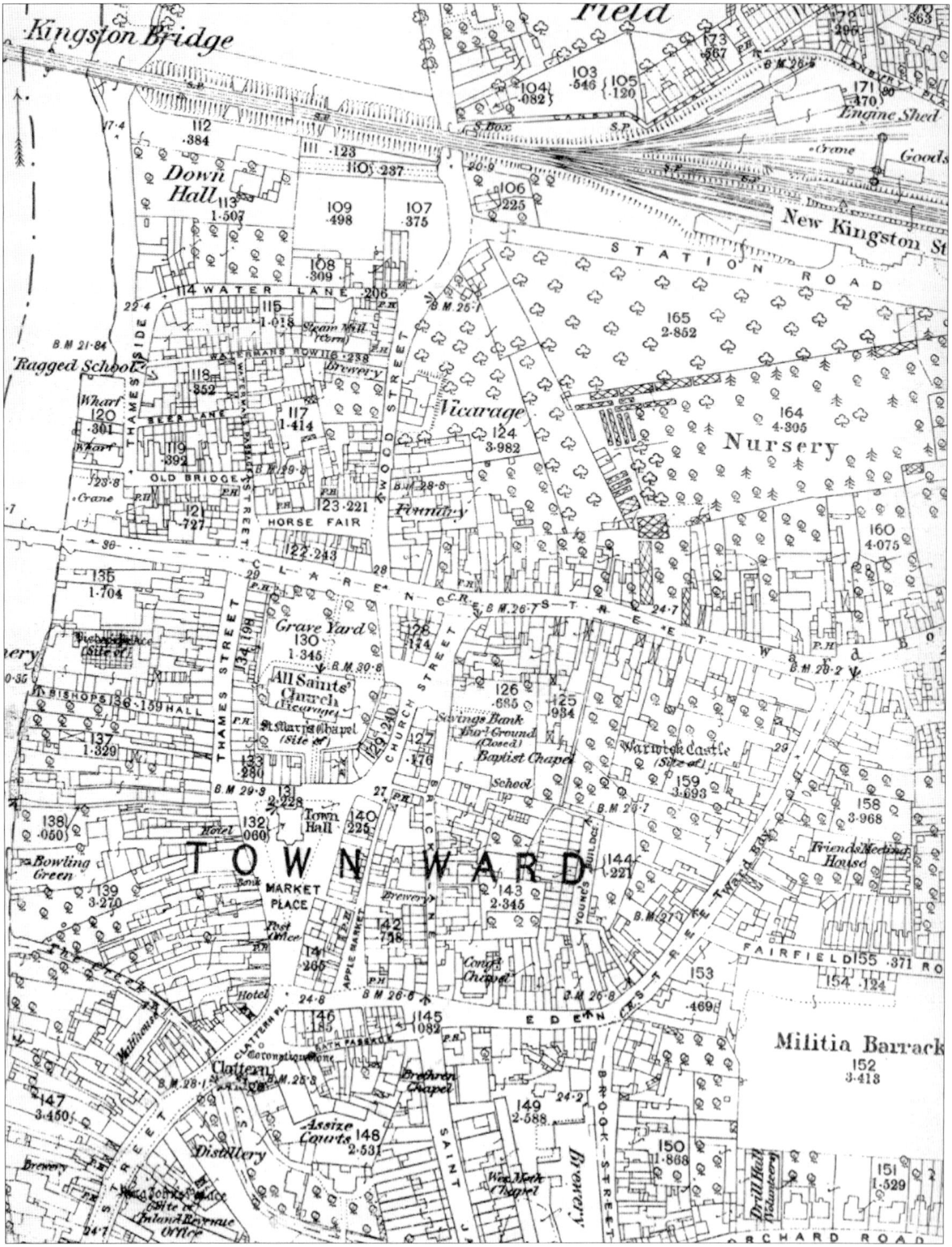

132. Ordnance Survey map of central Kingston, published in 1865.

to give Kingston official borough status, and Charles I's charter of 1628 giving it exclusive market rights over a seven-mile radius.

Such an extensive trading monopoly made it comparatively easy for Kingston to maintain the description given to it by the Tudor historian, John Leland, in 1535: "Kingeston is the beste market towne of all Southery." The seven-mile market privilege still applies to the new borough boundaries as extended by Royal Charter in 1965, though Kingston no longer exercises it.

Royal Kingston

There are only three Royal boroughs in England, and Kingston is the oldest. It was designated Royal by King Athelstan in 933. This was confirmed by King Edred who, in a charter of 946, referred to "the Royal town which is called Kingston, where coronations are accustomed to be performed."

King George V confirmed Kingston's Royal status in 1927, further consolidated by a charter of Queen Elizabeth II in 1964. This followed the amalgamation of the two former boroughs of Malden and Coombe and Surbiton to form the new borough of Kingston upon Thames.

The other two English Royal boroughs are Windsor and Kensington & Chelsea. Windsor was first designated Royal in 1965 and Kensington in 1899.

Technically, Kingston's Royal seniority entitles its Mayor to take precedence over all other English mayors (but not Lord Mayors).

133. St Agatha's Roman Catholic church in Kings Road, 1898.

134. St Raphael's Roman Catholic church in Portsmouth Road, c.1850.

St Agatha's church

Until 1894 the only Roman Catholic church in Kingston was St Raphael's, built overlooking the river in Portsmouth Road in 1847/48. But there was a pressing need for another when troops of the East Surrey Regiment returned to their barracks in Kings Road after service in Ireland, bringing with them several Catholic wives.

St Agatha's parish was founded in 1894. A year later

St Agatha's school was built close to the barracks, and immediately to the north of the present church. It was used as a temporary place of worship until plans for a permament church were drawn up by London architect, John Kelly, in 1898. The money for the new building was donated by Mrs. Caroline Currie in memory of her banker husband, Bertram Woodhouse Currie, who had died in 1896.

135. St John the Evangelist, 1873.

136. St Luke's church.

St John the Evangelist church, Spring Grove

St John's was founded in a temporary iron building in 1870, when Spring Grove, a rural area of glades and farmland, bounded by Hogsmill river, was being transformed into a housing area. It owed its creation to a wealthy miller named William Mercer, owner of the old flour mill which stood at what is now the junction of the Penryn and Denmark Roads. He was anxious that a parish church should be built in the new district during his lifetime and, as he was then 85, he felt there was no time to lose. He therefore gave a large site, and the then substantial sum of £2,500, with the proviso that both would have to be forfeited if a permanent building was not put up by 1872.

Mr Mercer died at the start of 1870, before even the temporary church was in place. Then began the race to build a permanent structure before the time limit ended.

The parishioners just met the deadline - the new church was consecrated in 1872 - but the enforced rush had lasting results. For one thing, the area was not yet ready for such a building. Knights Park Bridge was not built until 1894, and until then Spring Grove and its church were virtually cut off from the rest of Kingston by the Hogsmill. For another, there were not yet sufficient residents, and consequently not enough money to maintain the church. St John's has never really caught up. Uncompleted parts of the building, such as the intended spire, have never been finished, and though the building was designed to seat 800, the congregation has never reached that number.

Nevertheless it is a handsome building, designed by architect Arthur Phelps of Surbiton. In the 1970s Kingston Polytechnic, which has since evolved into Kingston University, began renting the church and its hall periodically for examinations, concerts and other purposes. That arrangement still stands, but the church is used for worship the rest of the time, and in 1976 - after fears that it might cease to exist as a church altogether - was combined with the neighbouring parish of All Saints.

St Luke's church

A principal feature of Kingston's Canbury area is its parish church of St Luke, which was built with the halfpennies and pennies of the poor when starvation and premature death were commonplace in the mass of houses that soon covered the former farm lands of Canbury following the opening of Kingston Station in 1863. Many people, both clergy and lay, literally gave their lives, by overwork and self-deprivation, to create and maintain this church, and today people come from miles around to worship in it.

One reason for this is its style. It is, in the words of those who established it, "the only church in Kingston to give full expression to the Catholic side of the teaching and ceremonial of the Church of England."

Its beginnings were in the 1860s, when a group of labourers and their families began meeting for prayer in a cottage parlour in Acre Road. Their parlour services continued until 1883, when they transferred to an old iron building that had been moved from its original site in Norwood and re-erected in Elm Road. The Bishop of Rochester came to lead the opening service and preach the first sermon, but though volunteers had struggled to beautify the building with flowers for the occasion, nothing could hide its shortcomings.

The Bishop did not mince his words.

"I see no reason at all why we should have cathedrals and beautiful churches built for the use of the high born, and think an iron church good enough for the poor", he declared in his sermon, adding that he hoped St Luke's would achieve a more seemly edifice within the next two decades.

He underestimated the new congregation. Only six years later on 14 December, 1889, he came again to St Luke's to consecrate the handsome brick building that has stood at the Gibbon Road/Burton Road junction ever since. Designed by London architects Kelley and Birchall, and built in red brick by W H Gaze of Kingston, it cost £5,139 – regarded as a great bargain even then. "It is a wonder to many that so much has been got for the money," remarked the *Kingston and Surbiton News*.

However, the church's most notable feature is the tower and spire, completed by Messrs Gaze in 1891, and given by Lady Wolverton to guide worshippers through a complex maze of streets to the new church. For that reason she stipulated it must be the highest building in Kingston; and so, until the late 20th century, it was. From the ground to the top of the gilt cross is a distance of 150 feet.

Brick spires are rare and this one, built of bricks made in Claygate, is the only one in Kingston. It measures 62 feet and is built on an 88-foot tower. The tower has two louvred windows on each of its four sides. Above these are circular apertures containing the dial plates of a clock described by its makers, the celebrated William Potts company of Leeds, as "one of the best ever placed in a tower."

The late George Ford, who at 95 vividly remembered the unveiling of the spire by Lady Wolverton, recalled in 1979 what a godsend the new clock was in a neighbourhood where the few fortunate enough to own a timepiece had to tell the time for everyone else. "People would relay a request for the time from house to house until it reached a clock owner," he said. "The information would then be relayed back, each neighbour passing it on to the next, sometimes the entire length of a road."

St Paul's church

St Paul's Church began in 1870 as a corrugated iron mission hut on the corner of Park Road and Elm Road. This was a rural area, still rich in arable and pasture land. Indeed, Elm Road was so named because it was bounded by fine trees. However, within 10 years the population had increased to 7,000 and St Paul's Mission District was made a parish in its own right.

The original iron hut had been erected and paid for by the Rev Arthur Cornford. He had been a curate in the neighbouring parish of St Peter's, Norbiton, but from 1870 was given the charge of the new St Paul's Mission. At the same time, he built and paid for the first St Paul's School, which still flourishes in handsome modern buildings in Alexandra Road.

With the British Land Company rapidly covering the district with housing, the iron building was swiftly outgrown. A site was found in Queen's Road, and in 1876

137. St Paul's church, Kingston Hill, c.1904.

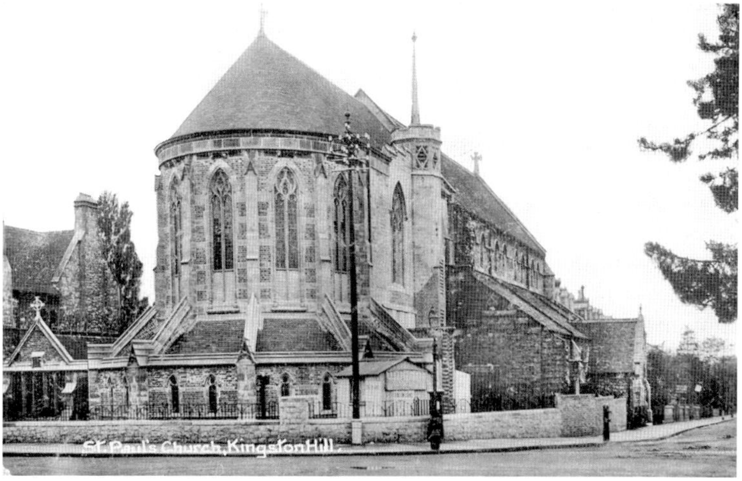

Princess Mary Adelaide, Duchess of Teck, laid the foundation stone.

No church in the Kingston Deanery ever took so long to build. Debts piled up on every side and it was more than half a century before the building was complete. Just how great the financial pressures were at that time is illustrated by the fact that, though enough of the building had been put up by 1877 for it to be used, the Bishop of Guildford refused to consecrate it until the debt of £1,500 hanging over it had been reduced. That task took three years, and it was not until 1880 that the church - still minus chancel, choir stalls, organ loft, transepts, ambulatory and side chapel - was consecrated.

St Peter's church

On the whole, Sir George Gilbert Scott could feel proud of his career. He designed, among several hundred other things, the Albert Memorial and the Midland Grand Hotel at St Pancras Station. He also renovated Westminster Abbey and Ely Cathedral, left a distinctive stamp on churches all over England, and achieved world fame. One thing, it is said, marred his sense of achievement – he was ashamed of St Peter's, Norbiton, which he had designed in neo-Norman style when still only in his 20s.

Today he would have no need to worry. The church is so hemmed in by flats, shops and Kingston's busiest main road that it is virtually impossible to get a complete view of it anyway.

However, that was not the case in 1842 when the building was consecrated. Norbiton was then an old-world country area, and the new church was a prominent landmark amid fields, farms, nursery gardens and noble estates. Its creation was a significant event because, until then, All Saints had been the only church serving the entire borough and beyond. The coming of the railways led to such an increase in the local population that a second church became essential. The result was St Peter's, the first ecclesiastical district to be cut from the ancient parish of Kingston.

138. St Peter's church, c.1904.

Whatever Sir George Gilbert Scott may later have thought of the design, it was better than anyone else could devise. For it was chosen from no fewer than 53 submitted plans, most of which the first vicar, the Rev. John Powell, dismissed as "miserable specimens."

The site had formed part of Norbiton Place, a stately home with magnificent landscaped gardens stretching from London Road to what is now the Cambridge Estate.

Norbiton parish is noted for its great size now. In 1842 it was even larger. For example, New Malden parish was yet to be formed, and there was no St Paul's on Kingston Hill, or St Luke's in Canbury. Mr Powell and his helpers therefore had to tramp miles over the unmade lanes of these localities. Carrying a lantern and a Bible each, often up to their knees in mud, they moved around the parish, holding 'parlour services' in workmen's cottages and conducting prayers at Kingston Workhouse (now Kingston Hospital) and Cleave's Almshouses.

St Peter's is still a lively force in its community, and has attracted a burgeoning Korean congregation in recent years. In 2005 it embarked on an extensive refurbishment to meet modern needs.

Sequah

In the autumn of 1890 a gold and scarlet carriage swept into Kingston Market Place and drew up outside the Griffin Hotel. Sequah had arrived, and for the next month an extraordinary frenzy gripped the town.

Kingston has had a colourful past. Royal coronations, civil war, plots and counterplots, the town has seen them all. But none roused more excitement and mass hysteria than Sequah, a dark and muscular man who was, he said, a North American Indian chief, bringing secret potions from the prairies to heal the sick.

Today it would be seen as just another PR stunt. To the Kingstonians of the 19th century it was nothing less than a modern miracle, and people flocked in their thousands to a field in Queen Elizabeth Road, where each night Sequah demonstrated his powers and pulled in a fortune from sales of his Prairie Flower and Sequah's oil. The first was said to cure all liver, stomach and digestive diseases. The second could, he claimed, heal the lame and cure the paralysed, and he set about proving it.

It must have been a dramatic sight. Every night hundreds of people pressed around his gilded coach while hundreds more, unable to get into the field, thronged the surrounding roads. Two huge spirit lamps, suspended on tall poles, threw a lurid light on the upturned faces of the crowd as Sequah swung into action. First he would appear on the carriage steps, forceps in hand, and offer to extract teeth free of charge. There would then be a great rush forward, the police allowing only one person at a time to mount the steps.

"In this way, about a couple of dozen persons passed under the operator's hands in about as many minutes," reported the *Kingston and Surbiton News*. "Several had two teeth drawn and one had no less than four extracted. All the time the band played."

Then Sequah got down to the real business of the evening. Anyone crippled with rheumatism, and unable to move without sticks or crutches, was invited to come into the carriage and be rubbed with Sequah Oil in the presence of two independent witnesses.

One by one the cripples were hoisted into the carriage, taken behind a screen and rubbed vigorously with the oil. In each case, after about 15 minutes' massage, they were able to throw away their crutches and run nimbly down the steps.

The *News* went on: "When Sequah presented himself at the door of the Griffin Hotel he found a crowd of people there, not only filling the street in front, but extending for a considerable distance into the Market Place and into Eden Street. No fewer than three bands arrived, and some 20 or 30 torches were lit. When Sequah stepped into his carriage he found that, instead of horses, about a hundred young men were standing in front of it holding long ropes with which they were prepared to drag him to the field. He was dragged up Eden Street and London Street to the field, the bands playing *For He's A Jolly Good Fellow*. The spectacle was not one easily to be forgotten. The field itself was literally crammed with people whose upturned faces, lighted by the powerful oil lamps on poles, struck the beholder with a feeling almost of awe, while hundreds of other thronged the road from a long distance away.

"At the conclusion of his business, the carriage was again dragged forth, torches were lighted and the return journey was about to be made when another object took up a position in the procession, and at once attracted much notice. This was a pair-oared gig, mounted on a van and bearing the name Sequah on its bow. It was decorated with fairy lamps, Chinese flags and passion flowers by the men employed by Mr A Burgoine, boat builder, as their tribute of respect for this modern miracle workers.

"A number of patients whom Sequah had cured were accommodated with seats in the boat. Behind this came about a dozen young men dubbed the Big Head Brigade, wearing huge masks. As the procession moved slowly along, it swelled in proportion and many persons witnessed its progress from windows and other points of vantage.

"On reaching the Griffin Hotel, Sequah would fain have alighted, but he was entirely in the hands of the crowd, who dragged him up High Street, along Portsmouth Road, up Brighton Road and Victoria Road and back to Claremont Road, St. James Road and Eden Street. About ten minutes past eleven, Sequah entered his hotel amid the cheers of a multitude of persons to be numbered only by thousands.

"Thus ended a demonstration for which it would be hard to find a parallel *within the annals of the town.*"

There were other extravagant examples of Sequah mania. But the highlight of his Kingston triumph was the athletic sports in which all the competitors were former cripples whom he had cured. The field in Queen Elizabeth Road was packed with a surging mass of spectators, while crowds and vehicles thronged the road for miles around.

"Each man was handicapped according to his age and infirmity," reported the Kingston and Surbiton News. "The scratch man was John Langley, the former paralytic whose wonderful restoration to health has excited the greatest comment. At a given signal they were off, each striving manfully to get to the front and going along at a pace which must have considerably surprised their friends. But the paralytic quickly outdistanced everybody else and returned to the starting point seven or eight yards in front of his opponents, the others behind pretty well together.

"Joshua Bennett, 70 years of age, a martyr to rheumatism was second and John Fasten, aged 74, who had suffered from the same complaint for seven years, was third. The first received a leg of mutton and the other two a 6lb joint of meat each."

Amid all this excitement, nobody seemed to notice a small paragraph in the local press reporting a meeting of the directors of Sequah Ltd. This revealed that there were no fewer than 23 Sequahs operating in England, and profits had been so great that still more Sequahs were being groomed to tour the US, Canada and India.

Kingston would not hear a word said against their idol. Doctors who denounced him as a quack were threatened with violence, while Platts Stores in Thames Street, which tried to undercut Sequah by offering its medicines at a reduced price, had its premises smashed up by a howling mob.

The following year, Sequah was exposed as a fraud by a magazine called *Hygiene*. It had analysed the miraculous Sequah Oil and found it consisted of two thirds turpentine, one third fish oil and a few drops of camphor. Prairie Oil was ordinary tap water mixed with carbonate of soda and aloes. Considering it cost two shillings (10p) for two ounces - a considerable sum in those days - one could see why Sequah Ltd could boast such handsome profits.

Hygiene's revelations made no difference to Kingston's faith in its medicine man, and he continued to visit the town for years afterwards. Charlatan he may have been, but who else can claim to have held such a grip on Kingston, now or at any other time?

R C Sherriff

Robert Cedric Sherriff (1896-1975) – always known as R C Sherriff – was born in Kingston in 1896, educated at Kingston Grammar School, and achieved international fame as a playwright, novelist and scriptwriter. He also became the highest paid screenwriter in Hollywood. He is particularly known for his play *Journey's End*; but he also wrote the scripts for such famous films as *The Dam Busters*, *Odd Man Out*, *Goodbye Mr Chips* and *The Invisible Man.*

But he would never have become a famous author had he not been a devoted member of Kingston Rowing Club. He says as much in his autobiography, published in 1968. For, though *Journey's End* is always cited as his first play, he had in fact written seven previous ones.

Sherriff recalled that he joined the rowing club on leaving the army in 1919. By 1921 the club's boats were beyond repair, and £100 was desperately needed to replace them. To raise the money, Sheriff and his clubmates decided to put on a play. However, they could not find a play with enough parts to keep everyone happy, so Sherriff decided he would try to write one. He had never written before, and it gave him a lot of trouble, but eventually it *was* put on and made enough money for the club to buy a new racing eight. He wrote six more plays for the club in this way, on the basis that the more tickets a member sold, the bigger the part would be written for him.

Sherriff loved being club captain but one day, to be gentlemanly, offered to resign if it was felt someone else should have a turn. To his intense disappointment, his offer was accepted. Handing over the minute book, he feared he would have nothing interesting to do in his spare time. It was then he started writing *Journey's End* to fill the vacuum. It was rejected by numerous actors and managers before being put on in London's West End, and then transferred to Broadway. The result was that Sherriff found himself earning £1,000 a week in royalties. Then Carl Laemmle, head of Universal Pictures, invited him to Hollywood to write the screenplay for *All Quiet on the Western Front.* Laemmle was so

139. R.C. Sherriff coaching a Kingston Grammar School eight in 1929, when his play Journey's End *first made him a household name.*

impressed by the young man that he offered him huge sums to stay in Hollywood; but all Sherriff wanted was to become a rowing master in an English public school.

Probably he would never have returned to Hollywood had he not failed to get a degree. He also failed to get a rowing Blue when an attack of pleurisy obliged him to drop out at the last moment. So he took up screenwriting again, and spent many years as the best screenwriter Hollywood had ever known, earning the then vast salary of £200 a day.

Sherriff died in 1975, leaving generous bequests to Kingston Grammar School. They include a share of all the royalties from *Journey's End* which, he stipulated, must be devoted to the School's rowing club. Those royalties were boosted when the play opened in the West End in January 2004, and enjoyed a hugely successful run until January 2006.

Street Names

ACRE ROAD derives its title from an ancient field name, Forty Acres and is a reminder of when fields extended from here to Ham Common. The opening of Kingston Station in 1863 raised the value of the land, and in 1868 trustees of the late Lord Liverpool decided to auction off the former Prime Minister's farm and its 193 acres. Much of the site was acquired by the British Land Company, who by the spring of 1869 had begun covering the fields of Park farm with residential streets.

BROOK STREET dates from at least the 13th century, when it was known as (H)Oggestrete – presumably because it led to the Hogsmill river, which until the 1930s flowed across the street. Wheeled traffic therefore had to pass through the Watersplash, as it was known, while pedestrians used a narrow iron footbridge. This dangerous situation, which resulted in several deaths and accidents over the years, ended in 1938, when the river was spanned by Bedelsford Bridge.

CASTLE STREET was named after Sydney Castle, a Kingston JP, and owner of Woodbines, a riverside mansion in Portsmouth Road where he entertained royalty. The Castle family had been shipbuilders and brokers since the days of Samuel Pepys, who mentions them in his diaries, and owned Long's Wharf at Woolwich and Baltic Wharf at Millbank. Woodbines has long since vanished – Surrey County

Hall was built on part of its site – but is remembered in the name of Woodbines Road.

CATTLE MARKET is so named because Kingston Cattle Market was transferred here from Market Place in 1925. It had been a weekly event since 1603 when James I, "desiring the improvement of the town and considering the good and laudable services hitherto often done to and bestowed upon us and our progenitors by the Bailiffs and Freemen", granted the town a Charter which included the right to hold a Saturday cattle market in which "all kinds of animals and live cattle, as well as horses, mares, colts, fat oxen, lean oxen, bullocks, cows, calves, heifers, sheep, lambs, hogs and other living animals of whatsoever kind, nature or species they may or shall be" could be bought and sold and the Corporation could levy tolls. The Cattle Market ended in the 1950s. But the tradition has continued with the general Monday Market, which still flourishes. The site was redeveloped during 1985-87 to provide an underground car park with an improved Monday Market space on top.

CLARENCE STREET was Norbiton Street, and later London Street, until the opening of the new Kingston Bridge by the Duchess of Clarence in 1827.

DOLPHIN STREET was created in the 1980s to link Wood Street and Fife Road, and named to commemorate the Dolphin public house which stood there until demolished to make way for the new thoroughfare.

DOWN HALL ROAD – *see* Skerne Road.

EDEN STREET Until Victorian times, Eden Street was called Heathen Street. A deed in the borough archives, which describes it as Hethenstrate, shows that had been its name since at least 1315, and it worried no-one until a prosperous auctioneer called John Dawson came to live there *(see Eden Street entry)*.

FASSETT ROAD. Thomas Fassett was a one-time owner of stately Surbiton Hall, where his daughter, Mary, was born in 1800. She never married but settled at The Grove, a comfortable old house whose 23 acres included a farm, orchard, paddock, lawns and pleasure gardens. The Grove fronted the east side of what is now Penrhyn Road. In Miss Fassett's time it was Grove Road, a pretty rural route bordered by fields and fine trees.

Miss Fassett died in 1861. Within days The Grove was up for auction.

"As a building speculation the situation, extent and other numerous advantages make it by far the most promising that has ever occurred, or can occur, in this locality," declared the advertisement. Most of the 23 acres were consumed by roads and substantial villas, but the developers paid their last compliment to Miss Fassett by naming one of the new thoroughfares after her. Meanwhile her house and a slice of its garden remained for another 90 years or so. Then it was demolished to make way for the ever-increasing development around Kingston Polytechnic (later Kingston University) Now the only reminder that it ever existed is the name Grove Crescent.

FIFE ROAD. Until the 1860s market gardens stretched south from Canbury Passage to Clarence Street, covering what is now the station and Fife Road. Then a new railway line was cut through the acres where the Fitt family had long grown produce for the London

140. The Grove in Fassett Road. It was the residence of Rhoda Broughton, the novelist, in 1895.

markets. The opening of Kingston Station in 1863 presented a golden opportunity for Thomas Jackson, a noted nurseryman. He cleared his land of glasshouses and nursery beds, and had the space transformed into a new thoroughfare, shrewdly seeing its potential as a direct route to the new station from Clarence Street and a valuable development prospect. He called it Fife Road in honour of his Scottish ancestry. Mr Jackson was deeply fond of his two unmarried daughters, and as a final flourish he built two houses, one for each of them, linked by a plaque inscribed with the single word SISTERS.

Years later the houses were converted into two shops, and their interiors totally re-modelled. But the plaque still remains in its original position, and puzzles many passers-by.

HIGH STREET was known for centuries as West-By-Thames Street. It was given its present name in the 19th century because of its commercial importance at that time.

KING'S PASSAGE There is a popular belief that this narrow footpath, got its name because monarchs of bygone centuries used it to get from Thames Street to the river. In fact it was named after John King, one of the most important men in early 19th-century Kingston, who had a drapery shop on its Thames Street corner.

(Confusingly, the same name has in recent years been used for another footpath, a few hundred yards to the north, which leads from the western extremity of King's Road to the riverside Canbury Gardens.)

141. King's Passage, then known as Sun Passage, leading to the river, c.1898.

KING'S ROAD, which runs east from Richmond Road to the Kingston gates of Richmond Park, was formerly called King's Highway. This was because it was kept in repair by the Crown after some long-ago monarch had taken it as a right of way across private land, presumably to give added access to the hunting territory of Richmond Park. In the 1860s the road was adopted by Kingston Council, widened and renamed King's Road. The same title was also given to the approach running west from Richmond Road to Skerne Road, previously known as First Lane.

KNIGHTS PARK derives from Henry Knight, who in the late 18th and early 20th centuries owned an estate on the south side of the Fairfield.

LADY BOOTH ROAD was originally Felders Lane, i.e. a place where felders, or rustics, lived. Later it became Bridewell Alley because of its proximity to the Bridewell Prison. It was only five-feet wide, and was described in 1861 as "a den of infamy with abodes of filth, shame and pollution." In 1864 the alley was replaced by Fairfield Road to provide proper access from Eden Street to the Fairfield. But nothing was done about the cottages. A townsman wrote to the *Surrey Comet* in 1866: "However great an improvement the making of a new road may be, it would have been preferable to have swept away the nest of hovels, for they are not worthy of the name houses, which teem with dirt and filth, and swarm with not too cleanly inhabitants."

Fairfield Road eventually lived down its infamous past, only to have all its buildings demolished for re-development in the latter half of the 20th century. However, its cleared southern side still serves as a temporary car park pending the proposed K+20 plan for a huge expansion of Kingston's shopping centre into this part of the town.

The name of the thoroughfare was changed to Lady Booth Road in the 1980s to commemorate the fact that the Salvation Army, founded by William Booth in 1865, had its Kingston Citadel here for many years. The name sparked criticism of Kingston Council's ignorance that Booth's wife, Catherine (known as 'The Mother of the Salvation Army') was *not* a titled lady! However, the mistake was never rectified.

PENRHYN ROAD, formerly Grove Road, was named after Surrey County Council's first chairman, Edward Leycester-Penrhyn. He was born Edward Leycester, but assumed the name Penrhyn to comply with the will of Baron-

142. Pratt's Passage. Water-colour by C B Harcourt, c.1890.

144. Down Hall in Skerne Road.

ess Penrhyn of Penrhyn Castle. He married a daughter of the 13th Earl of Derby, and spent four years as council chairman.

PRATT'S PASSAGE was created off what is now Clarence Street in 1823. It got its name several years later from a Mr Pratt, who opened a leather goods shop adjoining its eastern corner. Pratt's Passage originally provided a pedestrians' short cut to Eden Street. However, it was re-aligned in the 1980s to accommodate a major re-development scheme.

RICHMOND ROAD was formerly Canbury Lane because it ran through the old manor of Canbury.

SKERNE ROAD was Bar(re) Lane from medieval times to the 18th century because it originally led from Barre Bridge, built late in the 12th century to span a watercourse that flowed into the Thames. Both bridge and watercourse vanished long ago, and by the 19th century Bar Lane had become Lower Ham Road. In the 1980s the section between Wood Street and King's Road was re-named Skerne Road in memory of Robert Skerne. He was a wealthy 14th-century lawyer, who married a daughter born to Edward III and his mistress Alice Perrers, and lived in Down Hall, a riverside mansion acquired by Bentalls in the 20th century for a car park and other buildings.

VICARAGE ROAD was first known as Beer Lane, then Pheasant Lane from a pub of that name which stood on one corner. Later it was widened and re-named Vicarage Road because of the former vicarage which stood immediately opposite in Wood Street.

VILLIERS ROAD

This was formerly known as Oil Mill Lane because Chapel Mill, an ancient corn mill on its eastern side, was converted into an oil mill around 1776. Here oil was extracted from linseed, which was brought to Kingston in barges and taken to the mill on horse-drawn carts. The mill closed early in the 1880s to make way for a railway that never materialised. In 1895 it re-opened as a factory where the celebrated Kingston Candles were made until 1922. Today the corporation refuse depot occupies the site.

Oil Mill Lane became Villiers Road in the 1930s in memory of Lord Francis Villiers, younger brother of the Duke of Buckingham. He, along with others, was killed near here in 1848, fighting for the doomed King Charles I in what is generally described as the last armed engagement of the Civil Wars.

143. Skerne Road.

145. *The west side of Wood Street, at the corner of Water Lane, c. 1895.*

WOOD STREET

The section of Wood Street that runs east from what is now Bentalls department store and Kingston Station did not exist before 1860. Instead the area was agriculture land, where produce was grown for the London market. Then came news that Kingston was to have its own railway station, and much of the land was acquired by the London & South Western Railway Co. for the construction of the raised line, the station, which opened in 1863, and a new approach road. The new thoroughfare was named Ceres Road after the Goddess of Agriculture to commemorate the previous use of the site. This tribute to a chapter of Kingston's economic past was obliterated in 1936, when 'Wood' replaced 'Ceres' to widespread regret. The part of Wood Street that runs north from what is now Clarence Street is a centuries-old route that was originally only a few feet wide.

Surrey County Hall

The Surrey County Council building in Penrhyn Road looks a model of grand respectability. Yet it was once associated with effigy burning, fisticuffs and quarrels of the most violent kind.

It all began on 14 January, 1889, when Surrey organised the first meeting of elected county councillors ever held in Britain. At that time the council was meeting temporarily at Newington Court House, and soon a pitched battle began over where the council's permanent home should be. Kingston, Guildford, Wimbledon, Redhill, Epsom, Reigate and Little Booking were all anxious for the honour, and finally a special committee was formed to settle the issue.

The committee chose Wimbledon, but the decision caused such uproar that a ballot was held in which Guildford came top with 23 votes. In the next round, Guildford polled 23 votes, Wimbledon 18 and Kingston 17, Furiously Wimbledon demanded, and got, a recount, but had to concede second place to Kingston.

"Now came a tug of war and amid increased excitement the chairman rose to take the final vote," wrote the *Surrey Comet.* In the final count Kingston scored 42 and Guildford 27.

Jubilant Kingston Council

146. *Surrey County Hall.*

offered two sites, only to have them rejected. Their third proposal was accepted: a piece of parkland that had once formed part of a riverside estate called Woodbines. Here, fronting what is now Penrhyn Road, County Hall was built amid many arguments, and the first council meeting there was fixed for 13 November, 1893. It was a red letter day for Kingston, and to celebrate the Mayor entertained the entire council to a luncheon beforehand in St James's Hall. The affair ended abruptly when it was announced there would be no reserved seats in the new council chamber. Hurriedly guests left the tables, scrambled for their coats and raced to County Hall.

"Many, including peers and usually sedate country folk, running the distance in a manner more energetic than fitting" commented the *Surrey Comet*, tartly.

They arrived to find the doors of the council chamber locked, but they set up such a shout that the doors were opened early, and the members rushed in, fighting each other for the best seats. There was more excitement when the room was suddenly flooded with electric light – the first time a public building in the town had been lit by this wondrous means. Kingston Electricity Station had worked feverishly to be ready in time for this great day, and it succeeded. In fact, Kingston Corporation was one of the first municipal bodies to establish an electricity supply.

And the effigy burning and fisticuffs? The burning was at Wimbledon, where electioneering for seats on the county council reached a fanatical pitch. The fisticuffs were displayed in Kingston, where a mere tradesman named Alfred Higgs had the temerity to offer himself for election alongside county aristocrats and gentlemen.

"We cannot believe Mr Higgs is so puffed up with vanity as to consider himself a fitting representative for the town," said the *Comet*, outraged.

148. Interior of the Kingston Empire, 1910.

Needless to say, Mr Higgs was not elected.

Plans were more recently well in hand for Kingston University to buy County Hall, and make the building its headquarters as part of a £70 million redevelopment project. But in January 2006 Surrey's executive committee decided not to leave Kingston for a new base in Woking – an unexpected decision made to lessen rises in the county's council tax for the year.

147. The Kingston Empire in 1910.

Theatres

The history of theatre in the Royal borough is shadowy; but the few clues given by letters and memoirs show that at least as early as the 18th century, plays were being put on in barns and malthouses. For example, in 1749 the celebrated Horace Walpole wrote to a friend to say that some famous actresses were coming to dine with him at Strawberry Hill, his mock-gothic home at Twickenham, adding that "in the evening we go to a play in Kingston, where the places are twopence a head."

149. The Royal County Theatre in Fife Road, c. 1908.

The following day he writes: "I had not time to finish my letter last night for we did not return from the dismal Play, which was in a barn at Kingston, till 12-o-clock at night."

William Ayliffe, in reminiscences published in 1914, recalled how early in the 19th century "travelling companies of players gave theatrical performances in some old malthouses in Eden Street."

Old playbills show there was also a theatre close to Kingston Bridge at Hampton Wick. It described itself as "under the patronage of His Royal Highness the Duke of Clarence", and in May 1811 it put on two plays "by Desire of a Party of LADIES and GENTLEMEN of Norbiton."

Many productions were put on at the Drill Hall, built in Orchard Road for the 12th Surrey Rifle Volunteers in 1862. The first amateur performance of Gilbert and Sullivan's *HMS Pinafore* was given here in 1879 in the presence of Sullivan himself. Audiences of 1,500 flocked to the hall. But the building had no lavatories, with the result that adjacent roads became what the *Surrey Comet* disgustedly called "a perfect swamp."

In 1896 Peter Davey, a playwright living in Kingston, bought an old hall in Fife Road, formed a limited company, and built the 1,300-seat Royal County Theatre on the site. It cost £18,000 and opened in October 1897 with *Under the Red Robe*, which had just completed a successful London run at the Haymarket Theatre.

Here Mr Davey produced a new pantomime for 15 consecutive seasons. "They were entirely our own productions, and they became quite a local institution," he recalled in 1933. "The reputation of the Kingston Panto extended far beyond the Thames Valley, so much so I had offers of theatres all over the country, and one Christmas no fewer than seven Kingston Pantomimes were produced simultaneously at Plymouth, Brighton, Bath, Ipswich, Cheltenham, Croydon and Hull, in addition to our own new production in Kingston."

The Royal County did well until about 1908 when the motor car, trams and other means of easy transport began diverting people from the suburbs to central London. The growth of cinema also affected live theatre. Mr Davey ran his theatre at a heavy loss during its last two years. It closed in June 1912, and later became the Super Cinema – remembered by many as anything but super! Gutted by fire, the building closed in 1940, but was not demolished until 1955.

Kingston's second purpose-built theatre was The Empire, built on the site of an old mansion, Canbury House. All 2,000 seats were sold for opening night on 24 October, 1910, and it remained that way for years.

It also became a magnet for every major name in British showbusiness. Marie Lloyd, Florrie Ford, George Robey, Harry Tate, Vesta Tilley, Gracie Fields, Louis Armstrong – to name a few. It also launched Noel Coward on his world-famous career after he was taken to see the Empire panto.

"It was my first-ever visit to a theatre, and I decided there and then to make it my career," he said in later years. "Actually, I never saw the panto. The excitement made me sick. But it set the course of my life."

Empire audiences dropped sharply after the Second World War, and it closed on 16 March, 1955. The interior was then gutted for a supermarket. It was converted into a Wetherspoon pub in 1999 but much of its original exterior survives.

Kingston's third purpose-designed theatre, Rose of Kingston, has been dogged by controversy ever since it was conceived in the 1980s as an adjunct to Charter Quay, a riverside development of shops, cafés and apartment blocks. The shell of the building was completed in 2003 but, due to difficulties in raising the £8.5 million needed for its fitting out, the planned opening in 2004 could not take place. In 2005 Kingston Council raised public hackles by committing £3 million to the project, and the building was supposed to open in September 2006, with Sir Peter Hall as artistic director. There was further public rage in January 2006 when it was revealed that the theatre would not open until 2007 "at the earliest."

Inspired by the 16th-century Rose Theatre, whose archaeological remains were discovered in Southwark in 1989, Rose of Kingston will have a promontory stage surrounded by three tiers of seating (1,100 capacity).

150 & 151. The Tiffin schools, above for boys, and below for girls.

The Tiffin Schools

Thomas Tiffin and his brother were wealthy brewers in 17th-century Kingston, and Thomas served as a Bailiff (roughly equivalent to the later office of Mayor) in the 1630s. In his will of May 1638 Thomas left £50 to Kingston Corporation, with the wish it be used to buy lands or property, the income from which would be used to educate "some honest poor man's sonne" at "some good schoole", and then bind him out as an apprentice.

The following year John Tiffin left £100 for the same

purpose, and the combined legacies were used to buy land whose rents were spent on the education and clothing of children for the next two centuries. In the 1870s the Tiffin bequests were amalgamated with other educational charities to provide a boys' school, and later one for girls, both of which still bear their name. The Tiffin School opened in 1880 in new buildings designed by Loxwood King on the Fairfield. It was designed to accommodate 150 boys on the ground floor and 150 girls above, and the fees were £3 a year. As the popularity of the school increased, the problem of space became more pressing. This was temporarily solved in 1899, when the girls moved to new premises in St James's Road. By1910 space was again a problem, and it was decided to buy land in Penrhyn Road for new premises. Before the purchase could be completed, the First World War intervened.

Overcrowding in the boys' school was becoming intolerable when, in 1920, the eventual solution was first proposed. But it took nine years to materialise. This was the purchase of Elmfield, an 18th-century mansion with grounds bounded by London Road, Queen Elizabeth Road and Birkenhead Avenue. These were bought by Kingston Education Committee for £5,800, though conversions and additions were not complete until 1929. The school's Fairfield building was then acquired for St Joseph's Roman Catholic School, which opened there in 1935 and has continued there since.

Tiffin Boys' School is now a selective grammar school, with 1070 boys aged 11 to 18. It is among the top 100 schools in England, with official designation as a performing arts college.

152. Union Street Baptist chapel and the town mortuary next door, 1902. In the left foreground is the Fire Brigade's engine house. The mortuary, with a top floor added, is now a patisserie.

Two major developments in 2004 were the completion of the Dempsey learning resources centre and the Judge lecture theatre, both designed by IID Architects of Twickenham.

In 1937 Tiffin Girls' School left St James's Road for new, purpose-built premises in Richmond Road, and in 1987 moved next door to what had originally been Rivermead Boys' School, and later Tudor School. This building, set amid nine acres, was severely damaged by fire that destroyed half of its teaching space in December 2003. Nevertheless, the school kept going without a break, though some pupils had to work on a week-on, week-off basis, and lessons had to be radically replanned. A £4 million replacement building mainly funded by Kingston Council, was completed in 2006, with the school itself launching a fire appeal to pay for new equipment and furnishings. Despite these setbacks, the school was assessed in 2005 as the second highest performing state school in the country at GCSE level and is consistently in the top 25 per cent of all maintained schools.

Union Street

Charles Dickens' *Pickwick Papers* is one of the world's great novels. But one of its lesser-known aspects is that it played a part in renaming one of Kingston's oldest thoroughfares.

Union Street is a narrow road running from the Garden of Remembrance in Church Street to Eden Street. Up to 1834 it was known simply as Back Lane – a name often used in centuries past to denote a slum area of no importance. Presumably as the street grew in stature as a manufacturing and business centre, this name represented a real handicap. At any rate, it was re-labelled Brick Lane, and so it might have remained had *Pickwick Papers* not been published in 1837.

The book had first appeared in monthly episodes the previous year, and when it was published as a complete volume, it had one of the highest sales ever recorded. It was meant to be amusing; but members of the Brick Lane Baptist Church were incensed by a passage describing the affairs of "the Brick Lane branch of the United Grand Junction Ebenezer Temperance Association", and considered that it ridiculed them. Led by a Mr Ash, who owned a cooper's workshop near the chapel, they began a campaign

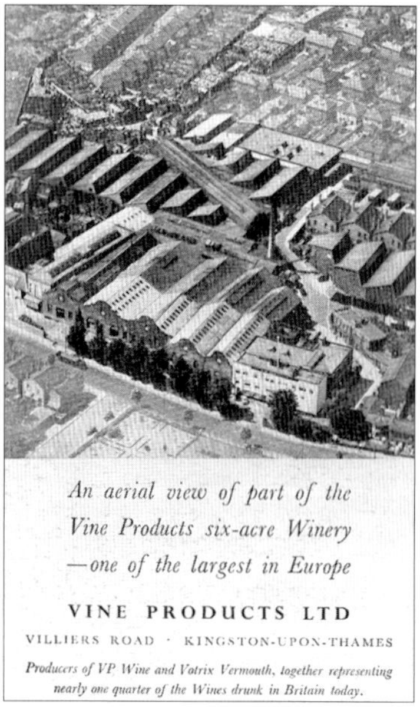

153. Aerial view of Vine Products, c. 1950.

to have the name of the road changed. They had little success until 1865, when one of their deacons, Joseph East, became Kingston's first non-Conformist mayor. Soon after that workmen arrived in Brick Lane and affixed two metal wall plates, one at each end of the road, bearing the name Union Street, in honour of the Baptist Union.

There was another reason why Kingston Baptists did not wish to be associated with a temperance association, fictitious or otherwise. For Brick Lane boasted three breweries, one of them owned by Mr East himself!

Vine Products

Much of the history of British wine took place in Kingston, where Vine Products (VP) had the largest winery in Europe until 1989. It all began in 1901, when the Mitsotakis brothers began making British wine from grape juice imported from their family vineyards in Greece. There was such demand that in 1905 they established Vine Products Ltd (usually known simply as VP) and in 1907 moved to a spacious former brewery in Kingston's Oil Mill Lane (later re-named Villiers Road).

Their early products were mainly cordials, liqueurs and the kind of brews that British housewives had made at home for centuries. Soon, however, British-made wines and sherries became the best sellers. All these pioneer lines were contained in barrels, made by craftsmen in the company's own cooperage. Not until 1936 were two bottling lines established with a total capacity of 12,000 bottles a day.

The company's decision to transfer to Bristol in 1989 meant the loss of 240 jobs and of the giant storage tanks - said to be the largest of their kind in the world - that were such a familiar feature of Kingston's industrial landscape. By then VP had captured 60 per cent of the British sherry market, plus 75 per cent of British-made wine sales, and was producing more than a million bottles each week.

Ironically, the company's final decade in Kingston was also its most interesting, innovative and successful chapter, following a revolution in its product development and marketing techniques. The first major achievement of the new look Vine Products was the launch in 1979 of Concorde, a sparkling wine that was the first of its kind in the British drinks industry. It established a record as the fastest growing new product ever to enter the British wine field, and was responsible for a significant growth in demand for light British wines. Other trail-blazing products were Mardi Gras and Belgrove in 1983; Lotus, a blend of British wine and fruit juice, launched as the first of its kind in 1984; and Concorde Peach, Gavriche (a chocolate cream liqueur likened to "Black Forest gateau in a bottle)", Rougemont, Castle Blush, Chiros and Seagers, all launched in 1988.

But the company's flagship brand was QC British sherry, launched in 1958.

In 1996 VP's eight-acre site was given over to a housing estate and only road names such as Winery Lane and Vineyard Close serve as a reminder of the great industry that once operated there.

Jacqueline Wilson

Jacqueline Wilson (b.1945), the UK's children's laureate, was revealed as British libraries'

154. Jacqueline Wilson.

155. *The dining room of the Kingston Union Workhouse.*

most borrowed writer in 2004 when Public Lending Right figures showed her books had been taken out two million times. Along with JK Rowling, she has also been voted children's favourite author and in a poll to find the nation's best-loved author, she came in ahead of Bill Bryson, JRR Tolkein and Charles Dickens.

Though born in Bath, she has spent most of her life in Kingston, where she was educated at Coombe Girls' School and developed her love of books in Kingston Library (she has more than 15,000 volumes at her home in the Royal borough!) .

She was appointed OBE for services to schools in 2002 and in 2005 became Children's Laureate. She is published all over the world, translated in 30 languages, and to date has sales of well over ten million.

The Workhouse

Kingston's first "house to employ the poor to work in" opened in the Horsefair in the early 1700s. At the time, according to a Kingston Council document, "the poor of the towne daily increase, and are becoming very burdensome to the inhabitants." Presumably the venture was inadequate, for at a vestry meeting in 1725, it was decided that as "the poor of Kingston are become very numerous and chargeable", it would be advantageous to set up a place where they could be "sufficiently maintained and educated and taught to work, read and write, and set to work in order to introduce amongst the poor habits of virtue, sobriety, obedience and industry and labour, prevent an entail of poverty and idleness and to keep the poor at work and from begging about the streets and pilfering and other vices and idleness."

This time the poor were housed in rented premises near the site now occupied by Surrey County Hall. They were obliged to wear grey uniforms and prominent paupers' badges, perform allotted tasks, and be punished with three days on bread and water if they misbehaved. The third workhouse was established in a 17th-century mansion in London Road *(ill. 156)*. There it remained until 1839, when it transferred to Kingston's fourth – and first purpose-built – workhouse. This was the result of the Poor Law Amendment Act of five years previously, which decreed that groups of parishes within a 10-mile radius should form themselves into local 'unions' responsible for the relief of the poor. Kingston Union was formed in 1836,

156. The third Kingston Workhouse, opposite the Coombe Lane junction in London Road.

and the following year paid £150 an acre for Farmer Dickens' field in Coombe Lane for a new building. After many setbacks it was completed as a large neo-Tudor building. It could accommodate 320 paupers, and was handsome enough to be dubbed 'The Grand Palace' by the irate ratepayers who had funded it.

Male paupers were employed in breaking granite, chopping wood and making clothes and shoes for the inmates, while women did domestic work and shirt and bonnet making. Each was given an outfit "to wear all day on Sunday" and allowed to change their stockings once a week.

But the main problem was the thousands of vagrants and 'tourists' who came to Kingston because it was the centre of the Poor Law Union and close to many race courses. Many relied for accommodation at a penny a night in squalid lodging houses. The rest looked to 'The Grand Palace' where, according to the *Surrey Comet*, some 500 a week were provided with bath, supper, bed and breakfast in 1873.

Of these, it was said, only 10% were genuinely seeking work. The rest were professional beggars.

There was much support for a *Surrey Comet* leader of 1880 which declared that vagrancy had become a social disease and workhouse relief too indulgent. "The housing of vagrants is so far superior to that of honest labouring men that the casual ward, with the comforts of warmth, good bedding, food and cleanliness forms part of a legalised system which has the effect of encouraging idleness and professional begging which are next door to crime," it said. Evidently conditions became tougher in later years. In 1897 a *Kingston and Surbiton News* reporter described a night in the casual wards. He told how new arrivals were given bread and water for supper. They had to rise at 5.30am for more of the same before the dreaded task of turning the pumps – the workhouse got all its water from a 60-foot well, raised by pumps and forced up a further 80 feet into tanks housed in a tower.

In 1930, Boards of Guardians were abolished and replaced by public assistance committees. The Kingston Guardians mourned the change, but had the satisfaction of knowing that the facilities they had provided over the years had evolved in the finest hospital in Surrey – the original workhouse buildings accommodated Kingston Hospital for the next three decades.

Zoological Farm

One of the lesser-known aspects of Kingston's history is that the Zoological Society of London kept and bred animals on Kingston Hill for its zoo in Regent's Park.

In 1829 the society purchased "a farm consisting of a house with some convenient buildings and about 30 acres of land nine miles from Hyde Park Corner, in a beautiful situation under the wall of Richmond Park..." Here, on a site extending from what is now Liverpool Road to a spot just short of the Ladderstile Gate to the Park, kangaroos "bred freely", along with several varieties of fowl, sheep, deer, lions and other animals, under the supervision of a superintendent, a head keeper, two keepers, two labourers and a nigh watchman.

Various trials were planned, such as breeding rare ducks and crossing zebras with asses, a Wallachian ram with Dorset ewes and Southdown ewes with a goat and a deer; but the results were disappointing. A probable reason for this was the large number of visitors authorised by Fellows of the Society. There is an indication of this in a letter from the superintendent, Mr Papps, explaining why he had refused to admit a group even though they had a Fellow's order.

He describes how "a party of 17 persons, introduced by a Lady of Title, dined on the lawn and amused themselves with hunting the zebras and kangaroos about – upsetting the coops and carrying the ducks about in their arms, and afterwards pouring Punch or something similar into their pans. The Men were kept till past 10 o'clock searching for the ducks after the Party had left, and seven ducks died the next day in consequence of the treatment they had received."

The farm also proved expensive to run, especially after a large stock of animals were transferred there from the Royal menagerie at Windsor. In 1834 the Society began selling off the land. In the meantime the reduced site was used as a hospital for zoo animals.

Further Reading

Anderson, A: *History and antiquities of the ancient town of Kingston Upon Thames* (1818)
Aubrey, J: *The natural History and Antiquities of the County of Surrey* (1718)
Ayliffe, G W: *Old Kingston: Recollections of an Octogenarian* (1914)
Bellars, Margaret: *Kingston Then and Now* (1977)
Bentall, Rowan: *My Store of Memories* (`1974)
Besse, J: *A Collection of the Suffering of the People called Quakers* (1753)
Biden, W D: *The History of Antiquities of Kingston Upon Thames* (1852)
Blackmore, L K: *A Biography of Harry Hawker* (1993)
Brayley and Britton: *History of Surrey*, Vol. 2 (1850)
Broome, H: *Kingston Union: The Beginning and the End* (1930)
Bryan, W C: *Bygone Memories of Kingston and Norbiton* (1932)
Butters, Shaan, *The Book of Kingston* (1995); *A House of Prayer. The History of St Peter's Church, Norbiton* (1992); *Kingston Museum 1904-2004* (2005)
Clarke, N J: *Adolf Hitler's Home Counties Holiday Snaps* (1996)
Clay, R M: *The Medieval Hospitals of England* (1909)
Cowie, Leonard: *A History of the Parish Church of Kingston Upon Thames*
Daley, Anne: *Kingston Upon Thames Apprentices 1569-1713* (1974)
Dendy, Marshall C F: *History of the Southern Railway* (1963)
Evans, Gordon and Ward, David: *Chantry Chapel to Royal Grammar School* (2000)
Finney, W E St L: *Medieval Games and Gatherings at Kingston Upon Thames* (1936); *The Church of the Saxon Cornations at Kingston* (1943); *The Borough of Kingston Ancient and Modern* (1902)
Fozard, J: *Sydney Camm and the Hurricane* (1991)
Godden, J S: *British Aerospace Presents 75 years of Aviation in Kingston* (1988)
Hardman, W, edited by S M Ellis: *The Hardman Papers* (1930)
Harley, R J: *Kingston and Wimbledon Tramways* (1955)
Harper, C: *The Porstmouth Road* (revised edn 1923)
Heales, A: *The Early History of the Church of Kingston Upon Thames* (1883)
Hill, Paul: *The Age of Athelstan* (2004)
Hillier, J: *Old Surrey Water Mills*
Howard, Adrian: *A Brief History of Wolverton Avenue* (2003)
Kellys' Directories
Kingston Grammar School: Quatercentenary booklet (1961)
Kingston and Surbiton News (1882-1900)
Kingston Upon Thames and Surbiton, History, Trade and Attractions in 1891 (reprint 1979)
Leeson, D and Woodriffe, B: *How Electricity came to Kingston* (1980)
Leland, John: *Itinerary of England and Wales* (2nd edn 1744)
Leyland Motor Corporation, Leyland: *Seventy Years of Progress* (1966)
Lown, S and Panizzo, P: *A Fair and High Locality* (1996)
Lysons, Daniel: *Environs of London* (1792)
McCormack, Anne: *Royal Kingston* (1988); *Kingston Upon Thames, a Pictorial History* (1989)
Merryweather, F S: *Half a Century of Kingston History* (1881)
Miller, Pat and Stephenson, Roy: *A 14th Century Pottery Site at Kingston Upon Thames* (1999)
Perkins, H H: *Bentalls, Over 80 years of progressive achievement 1867-1951*
Phillipson's Directory
Pink, J R: *The Excise Officers and their Duties in an English Market Town* (1995)
Pulford, J S L: *The first Kingston Quakers*
Robinson's Railway Directory
Robinson, D: *Craftsman's Art and Music's Measure* (1988)
Robinson, Isobel: *Spring Grove 1865-1880*
Roots, George: *Charters of Kingston Upon Thames* (1797)
Sampson, June: *The Highest Pinnacle: the history of St Luke's church and parish (1979); All Change: Kingston, Surbiton and New Malden in the 19th Century* (1985); *The Story of Kingston* (1972); *Kingston and Surbiton Old and New*; *Kingston Past* (1997, 2002)
Savage, J H: *Non-Conformity in Kingston* (1920)
Smeeton, C. *D: The London United Tramways*, Vol. 1: 'Origins to 1912' (1994)
Smiths Industries: KLG: *From Cars to Concorde* (1989)
Statham, R: *Surbiton Past* (1996)
Stenton, F M: *Anglo-Saxon England* (1971)
Sturney, A C: *The Story of Kingston Congregational churches*
Surrey Comet (1854 to date)
Wakeford, Joan: *Kingston's Past Rediscovered* (1990)
Wessex Archaeology: *Charter Quay – The Spirit of Change* (2003)
White, H P: *A Regional History of the Railways of Great Britain*
Whitelocke, D: *English Historical Documents 500-1042* (1955)
Wilkinson, B: *The Coronation's History* (1953)
Young, Harry: *The church in the Market Place – The Story of Kingston's Baptist Church* (1990)

Index

An asterisk denotes an illustration or caption